Brian Carter was born in .... still lives. He has been walking and climbing the British hills since boyhood. The author of nine previous books including *A Black Fox Running, Jack, Dartmoor — The Threatened Wilderness, Nightworld* and *Walking in the Wild,* he writes a daily country and conservation column for the South Devon newspaper, *The Herald Express.*

CARTER COUNTRY

Writings on Rural Devon

Brian Carter

CENTURY

LONDON   SYDNEY   AUCKLAND   JOHANNESBURG

First published in 1989 by Century Hutchinson Ltd,
Brookmount House, 62–65 Chandos Place, Covent Garden,
London WC2N 4NW

Century Hutchinson Australia Pty Ltd,
89–91 Albion Street, Surry Hills, Sydney, New South Wales 2010,
Australia

Century Hutchinson New Zealand Limited,
PO Box 40–086, Glenfield, Auckland 10,
New Zealand

Century Hutchinson South Africa (Pty) Ltd,
PO Box 337, Bergvlei, 2012 South Africa

Set in 11/12pt Linotron 202 Sabon
Photoset by Deltatype Lecru, Ellesmere Port, Cheshire
Printed and bound in Great Britain by
The Guernsey Press Co. Ltd, Guernsey, Channel Islands

British Library Cataloguing in Publication Data

Carter, Brian, *1937*–
Carter Country: writings on rural Devon.
1. South Devon. Community education
I. Title
914.23′5

ISBN 0–7126–2448–1

Contents

Introduction

For nearly six years Brian Carter has been contributing his daily column, 'Carter's Country', to the South Devon evening newspaper the *Herald Express*. Writing about wildlife and the rural scenes he knows so well, he has a wide following in his home territory.

The column not only brings the smell and feel of rural and wilderness South Devon to the reader's fireside, it also provides Carter with a platform to pound home the case for conservation and the environment. His voice is often raised against the overdevelopment of Devon but it can drop to a persuasive plea for voiceless creatures.

CHAPTER ONE

Seasonal Reflections

Wind on the Hills

Once, nearly 40 years ago, I used to run with the cloud shadows across Haytor Downs, trying to stay within one particular shadow for as long as possible.

Then, a windy day on the edge of autumn was pure magic. The billowing cumulus would sweep down from the north until sun and shadow had the landscape running towards the immense plain of South Devon and the small corner of the country where I lived. If I lay in the grass among the bilberries and heather the wind spoke to me in loud whispers and passed on its excitement.

On Leighon Tor I could look across the wooded valley of the Becka Brook and watch the flow of cloud shadows over Houndtor Down and Holwell with the sky enormous and birds crossing it like bullets. Then, the buzzard's skirl was an echo of the wilderness and the stampede of light and shade.

Down by the brook the trees roared and writhed and the water was broken into a mass of little hollows, like the hoofprints of cattle.

When I was a boy I was always the Red Indian, never the cowboy and the hills were my mother. The Indian had an affinity with the living world and the cowboy or American farmer was always the intruder.

Up on the hills on a windswept day I felt, as I do now, the landscape speaking to my spirit. The Red Indian was one of those pure animal men who padded through prehistory that ran like a geological fault into modern times.

They were refugees from Eden and for me Dartmoor was Eden, an absolute beauty offering sanctuary to the innocent and those who cared about the quality of solitude.

On the moors again last week the cloud shadows were in full flight and the wind was blowing hard. Just for the hell of it I ran with one of the shadows from Smallacombe Rocks towards Hay Tor and the past overtook me.

The Coastal Downs

I cannot remember another autumn when there were so few bullens.

Leaving the stony lane and the whitewashed cottages I walked on to the downs. Following the fence where the pasture ends and the steeps above the sea cliffs begin I examined the blackthorn but found no sloes, or bullens, as they are called in Devon.

The killing winds of February and early March were probably to blame but being a bullen lover I lamented their absence.

At the first shoulder of hill I stopped and sniffed the air. The faint stink of fox clung to the grass. It was one of those mornings of sea mist flushed with sunlight. The downs were dew-soaked and the ocean calm all the way to the great headland. I was warm in my shirt sleeves and own company.

Striding on I found the view opening up and familiarity in no way impairing the joy of being there with autumn busy all around me. Over the landslips which ended in beach, rocks and sea came the buzzards – those large brown-mottled coney hawks I always look for in this part of the world.

Whenever I'm away on business or returning down the motorway from a trip to the Hebrides or the Lakes I often summon up a vision of the downs; and then I see the buzzards and hear their skirling cat-calls in a place far removed from man's world of concrete and metal.

Eventually I came to the spacious summit of the downs to

meet the larksong and watch an immense flock of starlings drift like smoke into the coombe. Now a male kestrel was aloft and fidgeting to find comfortable anchorage on the sort of breeze that is incapable of blowing the dust off a butterfly's wings. Back came the starlings keeping low and sailing over the fields.

The mist thinned and the sun shone from a cloudless sky. I pulled the cagoule out of the rucksack, spread it on the turf, took off my shirt and sat facing the sea. Where the downs descended in steep grassy slopes into the coombe the rabbits were upright – their eyes on me. Above the beach and the cove the whiteness of the seabirds was accentuated by the dark-shadowed crags. The beauty of the morning was the beauty of the first morning.

Winter Thoughts

Yesterday evening I sat at the fireside with Christmas gone and the old year nearly spent and I thought about the winter that had only just begun.

A lot of people run away from Britain during the lean months in search of the sun. Looking back I remember how brown I was in April, May and June although last summer was a disaster in terms of sunshine.

Perhaps '83 and '84 spoilt us with summer temperatures up in the 90s and everyone living out of doors like Torbay was part of California.

Yet, as the needles fall from the Christmas tree and the decorations take on that After-Boxing Day droop, I regard the cold dark days to come with something close to excitement.

Love of landscape and wildlife have bred in me a love of the seasons and an eagerness to find beauty in all four: spring's plenitude, summer's fulsome warmth, autumn's splendid decay, winter's illusion of emptiness.

There is an ache in the air at dusk as you return from the lanes breathing the reek of kale after a mild, damp spell.

Then the wind stands between north and northeast and snowstorms flail down from Dartmoor.

The swift changes of weather are uniquely British – freezing fog, soft sea mist, showers, drizzle, frost, heavy rain, sleet, hail, blizzards, sun warm enough to bring out the butterflies – January can conjure up them all.

A West Country winter with Dartmoor behind us and the sea at our feet can be a mixture of Fauré and Wagner.

Unseasonal warmth and stillness can surrender without warning to snow on a wind that deadens the face; but whatever happens life manifests itself in the unlikeliest places.

Beneath the windowsills snails are slime-sealed in their shells against the cold.

Elsewhere survival takes on an urgency.

The haws have gone but the hips are there to sustain the birds when the countryside is gripped by an arctic freeze-up.

Holly remains to brighten Christmas because the birds prefer the berries after a frost or two has softened them up and added, perhaps, to their flavour. Meanwhile the scarlet berries on the bryony creepers are ignored by the birds sweeping across the skies.

Although the farmland may be comatose the winter sky is full of life. Wildfowl flight to Clennon Ponds.

Herds of swans flop down in estuaries, creeks and coves.

Fieldfares, redwings, bramblings, rooks, daws, finches, lapwings and golden plover flock together to quest for food, and when a clear frosty sky produces an unforgettable sunset immense congregations of starlings settle in the treetops.

Like the woodpigeon the native population is swelled by starlings from the continent. At dusk their aerial displays are awesome studies in precision which seem almost telepathic.

It is comforting to hear the mistlethrush, the stormcock, singing while snow whirls down. The robin and hedgesparrow are also in voice, competing against the rasping double notes of the great tit and the surprisingly loud twitter of the wren.

I listen for the blackbird's astonishing aria that a mild evening can suddenly free but the hush at day's end is usually left to the chaffinch, although the lark above the winter wheat is seldom silent.

Following the plough the black-headed gulls are not black-headed. A small dark cheek patch is all that remains of their summer hoods.

Among them the rooks look very black. By February this charming member of the crow family will be building.

Edward Thomas captures the essence of winter's end in his poem 'Thaw':

'Over the land freckled with snow half-thawed
The speculating rooks at their nests cawed
And saw from elm tops, delicate as flower of grass,
What we below could not see, Winter pass.'

A lovely thought but rather premature! It is difficult to think of an English rural winter without the rook cropping up somewhere.

I hated rook shoots when I was a kid. The sight of guns gathered beneath the rookery turned me homicidal and the discovery of an innocent old blacktop swinging from the keeper's gibbet had me swearing vengeance against the trigger-happy legions that roamed the fields.

A snipe drumming and a buzzard riding his roundabout of wind against the clouds make me happy, and greenfinches in a hedge full of Old Man's Beard delight the eye. They are celebrations of life.

An unashamed addict of 'handsome' weather I often pause on the Paignton–Torquay ring road and look across the hills of South Devon to the bottom of the sky and Hay Tor's white profile. I know then that Dartmoor will be clothed in beauty and mystery.

Once the snow ploughs have opened up the road above Bovey Tracey it is a privilege to wander round some white muffled village with the rest of the world remote.

Nearer home the winter lambing will be in full swing with its attendant hazards and hardships. The farmer can be pushed to the limit at this time of year as he patrols the pens.

All around Torbay the ewes are dropping young and the pens are full of birth-wet lambs. The low, contented grunt of mothers fussing over woolly scraps that bleat and fall about is a sound you would not normally associate with sheep.

Coming back one winter in the dark from a fox watch the whole night was happy with the smell of animal life. Frost gleamed by starlight and the hills of boyhood were alive.

A log shifted and coughed sparks. I pressed it down with my heel and fed some more wood to the fire.

On the rocking chair the tabby she cat stretched and subsided once more into drowsy limpness.

Now there were flower phantoms in the embers and I thought of the blooms January and February would offer not ironically or in defiance of harsh weather but rather as quiet evidence of the miracle we sometimes take for granted.

Winter flowers are a triumph for the strengthening daylight as January gives way to February. Coltsfoot and celandines among the young nettles in the hedge, the purple crocuses and purple iris with the snowdrop in the park say it all, wordlessly.

Yet the aconite rising above fallen snow does not move me like the pale lilac of iris stylosa.

The glory lies in all the apparent frailty of the flowers which frost, ice and snow can never smother. Roses budding in the garden, February's violets, grey hazel catkins turning yellow, toads, newts and frogs on the move – no demonstration of life within winter's illusion of sterility touches me so much as a glimpse of a solitary primrose in the corner of some sheltered South Devon coombe.

Perhaps half of winter's appeal lies in a heightened anticipation of what will happen come spring; but seated at the fire I found I was still in love with the season for its own sake.

Sunday Snow

How good it is to see my mother still going strong in her eighty-first year; still walking Tina the labrador to Goodrington Park, still feeding the birds in her front garden, still frying mushrooms and bacon in the kitchen where I saw most of my boyhood mornings.

She can conjure up vivid recollections of her Welsh childhood in the valley by the river where my grandfather took rich clients salmon fishing. The fierce vigorous ghillie stares out at me from the faded sepia of the photograph taken in 1915 when he landed a 47½lb fish.

'Big as him it was,' my mother says, again and again. She is small and wiry like her father with the independent spirit of a generation for whom debt was inconceivable and the work ethic prevailed above everything.

Dave Baker and I passed the terrace where she lives on the way to Clennon Valley in the snow of the last Sunday of February. The roads were already a brown and grey mess of slush, but we knew Clennon Valley would offer a pristine whiteness swept by the north-easter.

'We'll drop in for a cup of tea on the way home,' I said. Clennon lived up to our expectations. The wind funnelling between the two low hills had the kiss of broken glass. In places the snow was knee deep. Its surface was patterned only with the footprints of birds for it was too early for most people to be out walking their dogs. The wind that had brought the Arctic to South Devon was churning up the ponds and preventing them freezing. But the wildfowl and gulls looked desperate. Moorhen and coot paddled up in search for food and the mallard flopping down with kamikaze sang froid were equally insistent. Perhaps the mute swans were suffering more than the ducks or waders. The pochard and a solitary pair of teal kept to themselves among the half-drowned willows but the black-headed gulls screamed for food.

Out on the blanco'ed football pitches lapwings rose and cried and descended again. Dave and I looked at each other from numb faces and decided it was time for tea and toast.

'Come in, boys,' my mother said, like we were ten-year-olds and not a couple of middle-aged wilderness romantics in love with handsome weather.

'Sit by the fire and I'll put on the kettle. You're frozen stiff.' Forty winters were wiped out in a single phrase. Frozen stiff! She says that to my son and she said it to me when I used to come in from Curledge Street Primary back in those dark days just after Hitler's War.

Winter Valley

The first snowfall of winter brings a silence that takes us by surprise. Last week we woke to find the world transformed, whitened, stilled. Snow lay thin on a frozen surface and I came soon after daybreak to Clennon Valley.

Inching my way down Winner Hill Road I was overtaken by a dog whose headlong flight had become an out-of-control, high speed slide. The animal spun slowly as it passed, licking its lips and rolling its eyes. The postman creeping up the hill joined me in uncontrollable laughter and the crow on the roof of the garage said 'caw'.

All along Dartmouth Road cars were nose to tail at a standstill, puffing carbon monoxide. I marched resolutely past them to Clennon and came into the valley. Here the silence was friendly, because it fed on my past. All around me the tracks of birds and animals betrayed the secret life of the landscape.

The earth was hard under powder snow, hard as the iron in the carol, but the breeze left me with a stiff face and I could not sing the words: 'Earth was hard as iron, water like a stone.'

The pied wagtail walking across the pond understood what I wanted to say. Out on the ice, snow had been flattened to whorls by the wind. A mistlethrush sang from the undergrowth behind the pond, from the tangle that was once a lane.

Cattle grazed here during my boyhood. A voice thick with the Devon accent would call them in for the milking. My father was alive then and the leafless orchards were alive on the hill, although they slept through the dark cold months of fieldfare and brambling invasion.

I came to another pond with black-headed gulls crowding its edges. Many stood on one leg to conserve energy. Their cries curdled the bleakness to pain. Among the sepia stands of willow out in the water which was ice-free a great black-backed gull sailed among rafts of mallard and teal. Moorhen and coot voiced their disgust.

The sky was full of snow and had me thinking of Tunnicliffe's etchings. On the other side of Dartmouth Road the bulldozers were busy. Smoke billowed from scrub fires above the salt marsh. What had been was going up in flames.

The rush of water over the weirs broke winter's deadlock. A crow rasped. Duck called. Then with a sound louder than the weir the fieldfares exploded from the wood, massed, and flew off over Penwill Way. I crouched to probe the cat-ice filming the shallows of the pond and the cob mute swan tapped my boot with his beak, demanding food.

Because there is no obvious sign of soul-searching in voiceless creatures it does not mean there is no soul. This assumption springs from our arrogance. The black-headed gulls watching me with a nervous shift of the eyes confirmed this. We bring misery and death. We are the Lords of Death and wild animals recognise the demons we carry in our hearts.

I returned to the ponds at dusk and fed the swans and ducks. Rats scurried from the flags in the drainage gut and the valley was masked in the smell of woodsmoke from the fires over the road. There was a little fire in the sky above Clennon Woods to salute the setting sun, and the cry of herons rang through the trees.

Then, over and over, the melancholy hooting of tawny owls, poignant enough to resurrect passages from Thoreau's *Waldon*, which I had read before my eleventh year.

At 5.15 the 'prook' of moorhens joined the owl chorus. Crows rasped and duck swam briskly up and down the top three ponds which weren't frozen. How strange that these sights and sounds should carry me back to the winters of my boyhood, to firesides and faces which survive in dreams. Afternoon had smoked away to dimpsey.

The wind was moving in a wall of ice to break around me, chilling me with its splinters. Lapwings flew silently over my departure.

The next morning I came again in the drizzle to feed the birds. The swans snatched the pieces from my hand and even the cautious black-headed gulls clamoured to be fed. Presiding over breakfast was the constant arrival and departure of teal and mallard. Up on the top pond a pack of teal drifted among the willows, delivering their short musical whistles and ignoring me.

A heron flapped out of a sallow. The rain had stopped and morning was breaking bright. Beside the water I found a scattering of tiny grey-blue feathers where a sparrowhawk had defleshed a chaffinch. Light dilated and flared.

There was a keenness in the air. I examined the tracks at my feet; gull and duck prints, dog, fox maybe, voles, stoat, rabbits, crows. Well, we are all on our way to somewhere else, but animals never demand from nature what they cannot give themselves.

CHAPTER TWO

Village Life

The Village Street

Weaving between the houses, the village street bears witness to the past which hasn't been forgotten or erased as it has in many urban areas. The validity of this community's past is apparent at either hand.

The nearby Post Office Stores carries the name of a local family whose ancestry runs as deeply into yesterday as the roots of the oak you passed coming into the village. The two pubs, the church, the farms and cottages belong to another age but they sit comfortably in this environment where history hasn't been mugged or totally annihilated by catch-penny development.

Some of the walls are the original cob and straw; others are pink-washed. There isn't much thatch but there are good mossy weather tiles and roof tiles and narrow little porches and gardens full of begonias, geraniums, pinks and roses. Jackdaws and pigeons perch on the TV aerials and young swallows and starlings are wobbling on the telephone wires.

The street is liberally sprinkled with cattle dung. Flies swarm to the rivulets of warm urine left by passing cows. All the ingredients of the townee's rural dream are here, but the street has its own uncontrived character which depends on former realities.

The born and bred locals share the public bar of either The Royal Oak or The Dew Drop Inn with the new villager, the commuter.

It would be both stupid and arrogant to dismiss the hybrid lifestyle with a sneer as pure escapism. No one is escaping from anything. I search for tranquillity and the rural past isn't escapism any more than returning to the beauty of the living world is escapism. Maybe it's the conclusion of a conscious or unconscious quest for old realities.

I am glad I can walk this street and meet the Devon accent on the corner. That burr sits well on an afternoon disturbed by nothing more obtrusive than the shrilling of swallows and the growl of a tractor. Yet the street is part of a great factory devoted to the production of food. The milking herd plods by, water hisses from a garden hose, a dog barks, children's laughter gusts down from the village school playground.

At the end of many a summer's day throughout my life I've come to The Royal Oak and sat outside on the bench with a sleever of ale listening to the swifts and watching the butterflies on the flowering privet. Then I've beat a hasty retreat to the bar as the flying ants have swarmed on the queen's nuptial flight.

In where the accents are broadest I've watered my redsoil roots. Sitting on the settle looking out of the window at the light fading in the sky I know for as long as I breathe I'll be a Devonian.

Around the Village: The Cottage

The great boom in English cottage building occurred in the Elizabethan age, but I like the lovely austerity of South Hams cottage architecture which owes a lot to the Victorians and the weather.

The pink-washed cottage and its thatch are Devon – picture postcard Devon – but the weather-tiles and low shallow porches of the farm labourers' dwellings set in a row beside the village street have that authenticity about them which conjures up memories of boyhood summers.

Naturally I like honeysuckle and sundials set beneath a sweep of new thatch, but I grew up with farmworkers' kids and went into their homes which weren't that different from my own terrace house.

The lav was up the yard next to the ferret hutches and the chicken run. There was no bathroom and the scullery lacked almost all today's mod cons. Romance was absent from this way of life, but there were compensations.

A modest cottage now in a South Devon village costs a lot of money and the irony of the business wouldn't have amused my gran. The car has opened up village life to the outside world and urban expansion and urban pressures have made rural isolation attractive.

More and more people are escaping back to a pastoral reality even if their livelihood depends on the town. A minority are trying to lead an entirely self-sufficient country life.

The cottage can reflect different lifestyles, different attitudes to the same situation. There is the controversial holiday home and the second home which is perhaps a worthwhile addition to the village because someone may have rescued a derelict building and given it life again.

Then there is the house that is lived in all year round. Its chimney smokes in the autumn and winter, washing flaps on the clothes line, cats lie on the front doorstep and old folk tend the flowers or young children play in the garden.

In some of the villages I know generation after generation of Devonians have occupied the same properties and attended the one small village school before carrying on as their forefathers did or leaving the community.

Those cottages supplied the bulk of Stoke Gabriel's Premier Division side when I played soccer for the village in the sixties. Similar dwellings on housing estates and farms continue to fill Harbertonford F.C.'s team sheet season after season.

The cottages remain although people come and go. And between the rooftops and the churchyard the seasons pass, full of beauty.

Around the Village: The Shop

The doorbell tinkled and I came in out of the sunlight that had the cats rolling in the dusty street and the swifts flying high.

The shop hadn't changed much since my childhood. It had a low front, small windows and a door with a brass handle. A lot of village shops seemed to be run by single ladies or widows when I was young.

"Ere,' Aunt Vi would say. 'Pop down the shop and ask Miss Murch to let us have some sugar. And 'ave her got any starch.'

A working village isn't a museum assembled to attract tourists. The past shapes the present. It has dignity and value and the shop Miss Murch owned is still very much a part of the community's life.

In my boyhood, hygiene laws were pretty slack but no village shop was like Miss Hannaford's up the road from our terrace. There her grossly overweight cat, Piddly Seb, loosed his hair to fuzz the humbugs while the mice used the sacks of oats and rice as snack bars and lavs.

At the tinkle of the bell the old lady would brush aside the curtain that divided the shop from her parlour and sail out to take her place behind the counter.

Miss Murch kept a spotless little place. 'What the neighbours think' probably governed her life as it governed Aunt Vi's and the rest of the community. My mother used to say if you cared about people you talked about them.

At Miss Murch's money, goods and gossip changed hands. It was the way of that parochial little world and for many it remains more preferable to the cold indifference and neglect which can be encountered in any large town or city.

So the other week I came into the shop that had a bit of everything on its shelves from Cornish new potatoes to jelly babies, pork pies and the *TV Times*. The service was polite and the right pace for the establishment and its regular customers.

It isn't unfair to set this against all the elbowing and hurry you cop in town. There is the human touch which should never be undervalued as consumerism steam rollers politeness and consideration into the ground.

The couple who served me were courteous and I came away satisfied. Olde Worlde Charme has real relevance in these situations. It ceases to be a thatched cliché once you encounter it outside the country holiday brochure or TV village comedy.

In my town there are similar pleasant little shops – family-owned delicatessens, bakers, greengrocers – but for all their warmth you couldn't walk out of them into the cawing of rooks or the sight of three farm dogs running up the road behind a tractor.

Village Events: The Garden Fete

The fete in aid of the Misses Crowley's Friends of British Lighthousekeepers, was held on the lawn of Aishwell Court with Colonel and Mrs Redfern in attendance. A lot of old country families lent their support, although the charitable work was rather vague and the recipients themselves were often baffled by the Crowley sisters' parcels and hampers.

Mrs Redfern had knitted a lighthousekeeper's pullover herself and seeing it before it was packaged up the colonel said she was very clever to make it big enough to accommodate three men. Such a woollie was important survival gear. No lighthouse should be without one, he said, but perhaps the five foot arms were a little too generous.

The Crowley's endeavours brought many strange and wonderful things to British lighthouses – pullovers, gloves, scarves, books of poetry, bottles of claret, tins of asparagus tips, soup, Sherlock Holmes anthologies and boiled sweets. The fete would help ensure the flow of these essentials to the 'gallant exiles' as they were called by the Crowley circle.

The colonel had devised all sorts of interesting games and competitions to boost the funds and keep the guests amused. There was the Croquet Long Shot and the archery and the fly casting and the Guess-the-Pig's Weight and the Stand-on-One-Leg.

The WI sold buns, cakes and pies, and there were raffles for a Sunday dinner, a capon, a goose and a ride in young Nigel Redfern's sports car. Guests could buy lemon and barley water, strawberries and cream, salad sandwiches and ices at the stalls.

The Aishwell handbell ringers performed and the village children did folk dances and Mr Scott who had been in the mercantile marine played his accordian while his wife did the hornpipe. Mrs Redfern read selected passages from *Pickwick Papers* in the tent used alternatively by Madame Zodiac, the celebrated astrologist, and Madame Fortuna, the famous palmist.

Aishwell's guides and scouts demonstrated their skills in survival on the terrace and the Amazing Arturo, the ventriloquist, brought his dolls alive in rapid succession. All of them wanted a 'gottle of gear'.

The sun shone from a cloudless sky, birds sang and the rhododendrons reminded the colonel of his days as a subaltern in India.

The whole village mingled with the gentry on lawns as smooth as billiard table baize. In fact the only glum face in the crowd belonged to old Harry Blunt, the Redferns' gardener, who fretted about his lawn and all the tramping feet.

Arm in arm the Redferns strode through the crowd,

inclining a head here, smiling there, embracing someone of their own set or shaking the hand that belonged to a villager the colonel had known since childhood.

'A fete accomplished,' the Strutton boy said mischievously and the Redferns laughed.

Village Events: The Cricket Match

The Aishwell v Cornleigh match was the highlight of the cricket season.

In the summer of 1953 the rival clubs were celebrating the 50th Anniversary of the event and both were desperate to win the new trophy donated by Col Percival Redfern whose family had lived at Aishwell since the 16th Century.

Pc Stone was one of Cornleigh's trump cards. He bowled an accurate-medium pace, but Cornleigh's batting was 'woefully weak' (to use the favourite phrase of the Lansworthy *Clarion's* cricket correspondent).

Fortunately Aishwell could rely on the vicar's son who opened for his public school and the Langford brothers who had the village butcher's shop and were fast bowlers of repute.

The cricket field was one field away from the road. On one side lay Pincher's Copse, on the other the stream and the cider apple orchards. At the top was the pavilion and the old hunt kennels. At the bottom were the gardens of a row of farmworkers' cottages.

The July Saturday was all a lover of the game could wish for. It was the fifth day of the heatwave and swifts were screaming high on the wing.

Then, as the Aishwell team prepared to leave the public bar of the Drover's Arms, Fred Long, the scorer, broke the bad news.

'Cornleigh's got a new player,' he said. 'A batsman.'

'The Langford boys'll have 'ee,' someone grinned.

'Not this one,' said Fred. 'They got Plantagenet Hunter opening for 'em.'

'Plantagenet Hunter the county cricketer?' whispered Reg Langford.

Fred nodded and said 'He's tipped to play for England in the next Test match.' 'Get home do!' said Frank Langford.

'Tez true,' Fred persisted. 'He's staying at Cornleigh for a week – for a bit of fishing and a break from business. His wife's a smart party.'

Aishwell won the toss and put Cornleigh in to bat and glumly waited for the great man to appear. Plantagenet Hunter was a handsome figure. He had a Douglas Fairbanks moustache and Errol Flynn's smile and a Cambridge University cap and his gear was immaculate.

Watching him leave the pavilion Walter Zeal, the Aishwell captain, prayed for a miracle – and his prayer was answered by Sid Steer's large moody mongrel.

It was a cross between a wolverine and a cement mixer and it took an instant dislike to Plantagenet Hunter.

Before Mrs Zeal could react it had leapt the enclosure fence and was on Hunter like one of the hounds of hell. The poor man screamed and tried to beat off the dog with his bat. But Zeal's mongrel bit his hand so hard you could hear the bone crunch.

Plantagent Hunter retired hurt and the Langfords joyfully set about the rest of the Cornleigh team, skittling them out for a handful of runs.

'Dog Stumps Devon Star,' wrote the *Clarion* cricket correspondent. 'Aishwell win the Anniversary Cup in style.'

The dog Jim was made an honorary club member.

Yesterday's Villagers: The Innkeeper's Dog

Old Man Lazewell had a collie-cross with a dead blue eye and the temperament of the devil. Although she was tied up in his yard close to the shed where he kept the stock she would occasionally break free and wreak havoc in the village.

She had savaged the postman and attacked stray drunks and kept the back of the pub free of cats. Old Man Lazewell didn't care about his dog or his pub. He had given up and was dawdling through the last years of his working life into an old age he would devote entirely to self and idleness.

He always appeared behind the counter in his shirt sleeves and waistcoat with a seven day stubble on his chin and clues to his breakfast, lunch and dinner on his shirt front. He had a big nose and tired eyelids and a sarcastic smile; but his public bar was always packed with regulars because almost miraculously he kept an excellent draught Bass.

The fire was generous, too, because Old Man Lazewell hated the cold. Mrs Lazewell had left him years ago and was living with the breadman's cousin in Newton Abbot. The couple had been childless.

Lazewell's pub was devoted to the trade's basics – beer, cider, whisky, darts, euchre and gossip. The collie-cross who lived such a miserable, lonely life was spoken of with affection by the men who drank at Lazewell's.

'Careful,' they'd say to a naughty son or daughter. 'Mind your mouth or Lazewell's dug will 'ave 'ee.'

When they crossed the yard to the lavatory the poor creature would run out of length of her rope and snarl and bark with every hair on her body stiff.

One day she broke free and killed four of the neighbour's fowls before taking to the fields. Fearing for the lambs a search party went after her with guns to make sure it would be her last fling. But they never found her and she didn't return.

Maybe she met someone who wasn't afraid of her and showed her a bit of kindness or maybe the woods and fields were to her liking. She was an animal that was never weighed for her own worth. I hope she found peace and liberty, and didn't end up in a snare like everyone said.

Yesterday's Villagers: The Poacher

There was no romance about Albert. He was a big man with rosy cheeks and a beer gut, curly black hair and the cold eyes of a herring gull.

In the village he was known as Albert the Handyman because he could do all the little jobs around the house which the middle class found impossible or disliked. He could paint doors and gates, build a brick wall, mend a drain, kill chickens and cut hedges. Albert did very well, what with his smallholding and the poaching.

'He's a crool old devil,' my auntie said. 'I woan have un in the house, no zur. He doan care for ort.'

Albert had two Jack Russells and a big mongrel that could run down rabbits. He was a snare and gin man although he sometimes lamped pheasants and hares and used the 410 and 12 bore. There was about him an air which was both furtive and sycophantic. His cap came off and his smile came on as soon as he saw someone of 'note' and that smile became a half-leer whenever he confronted a woman who wasn't his social superior.

Albert tilled his gins in the hedgebanks and set his snares in the three big fields on the north side of the coombe. Me and the two eldest sons of Mr Blain the pigman at Lower Barton got to know his trap lines. We were 12 years old and I was already acquainted with the Clennon Valley poacher, Tacker. Like him, Albert was a clinical killer.

He moved among his snares, wringing the life out of the victims as they squirmed in his fist. His house was full of dead creatures — hanging pheasants, partridges, gutted hares, ducks, pigeons, rabbits. Albert rarely came back from a trip to the fields without the blood of a wild creature on his hands.

Me and the Blain boys would sometimes raid his traplines. We used to free the rabbits which were still alive and steal the dead ones; but Albert grew wise to our ways and lay in wait one morning before dawn. Then he ambushed us and caught me and Roger Blain and laid about our heads with his knuckles. Mr Blain had no sympathy for us. He was a countryman and had the occasional hare or bird from Albert. I never told my dad because I knew he would exact some bizarre revenge.

Whenever I hear a rabbit scream now under a stoat or a farm cat my mind flies back to summer nights and the awful sounds rising from Albert's trapline.

Yesterday's Villagers: The Farmworker

Ernie was indispensable to the farm. He was Jack of all Trades and the master of them all.

He could milk a cow, shear a sheep, mend a tractor engine, harness a workhorse for the wagon or machinery, plough, harrow and hedge. For this expertise he received a small wage and lived in a tied cottage.

The farm was small and Ernie would not have been there if the farmer's son had not been killed in the war and the other son hadn't married a farmer's daughter and gone off to her father's place.

Ernie was a hard little man, respected in the village and well-liked in Lazewell's pub which he visited on Friday and Saturday nights.

He had ginger hair cut in the short-back-and-sides fashion of the day and he always wore black leather boots and heavy cords. Ernie's three daughters loved him. They were all in their teens and had their dad's carrot hair and bony frames.

Two were at school and the eldest worked with Ernie's wife at the Big House. Ernie's garden was remarkably productive. He grew the ingredients of stews and kept fowls and ducks. His border collie was a sweet old bitch called Sally.

At the back of his house were ferret hutches and the wood stack. Ernie was an honest, intelligent countryman with little to say. His Devon accent was often mistaken by visitors as a sign of a slow mind, yet he could take a bit of wire and tinker with a tractor engine and get it going when everyone else had failed; and his knowledge of animal husbandry was encyclopaedic.

The farmer had great regard for him although he rarely showed it in case Ernie demanded a wage above the union rate. But farm work was Ernie's vocation. Given the opportunity he could have run his own place without much trouble but he was content.

He grew his own food, cared for his few animals and accepted his lot with little complaint. When he spoke in the pub everyone listened for he had the respect of the community. He was honest and industrious and was no threat to the social order of things within the village. The land gave him everything he required.

Yesterday's Villagers: The Doctor

I could run across the countryside into another world — a gentler, green world where life seemed to pass at the leisurely pace of a cow. The village wasn't far away and I knew most of the kids.

There was the class affinity, the ragged trousers, the grime and the catapults, the swearing and the veneer of hardness.

Those were the Iodine Days when every cut received the dreaded treatment. I remember tearing my leg open on some loose corrugated as I jumped between garden sheds. The doctor was called and he got out the dreaded brown bottle.

Although I was never a 'signed-on' official patient of this kindly old gentleman I got to know him throughout a wild childhood and wilder adolescence. Maybe nostalgia has helped create a saintlike figure but I believe, and my contemporaries confirm it, that he was special. He presided over the well-being of the small rural community for decades with patience and compassion. His humanity was faultless and he was that rarity – a genuinely good person.

This did not stop me on occasions from raiding his gooseberry bushes for the heavy purple gogs which were loaded with succulence. The Victoria plum tree outside his surgery also tempted me and on one embarrassing occasion he caught me up it filling my shirt front with fruit. He retrieved the plums and sent me on my way, feeling like Attila the Hun caught nicking pearls from the Pearly Gates.

The doctor was old when I was at primary school. He died in the early 1950s, mourned by an entire parish. If they had held his funeral in Westminster Abbey the place would have been packed. But people like the doctor don't get into Westminster Abbey or St Paul's Cathedral. Those places are reserved for poets and statesmen and soldiers – the 'heroes' of the nation.

The doctor brought hundreds of children into the world, comforted generations of sick villagers and helped many old friends to make a calm exit from this life. When he was young he cycled around the farms in all weathers, he attended pregnancies in blizzards and he worked long hours, year after year. His grave is marked by a small granite headstone in the village churchyard.

Driving towards Bristol the other day I saw the Wellington monument on the skyline and I thought of the doctor and of all the other real heroes that get into people's hearts but not the history books.

Yesterday's Villagers: The Postman

Ralph's round was big even by rural standards. It included over a score of outlying farms, some of which were reached by muddy cart tracks. One was almost at the top of Victoria Beacon where a fire had been lit as part of the Old Queen's Diamond Jubilee celebrations. Another was in a coombe the other side of the water splash which became impassable after heavy rain.

Ralph liked his job. He was his own boss when he took the van on to the road but he went to great lengths to see that the King's mail got through. His determination was apparent on the football field. He captained the village team in Division 2 of the South Devon League and never flinched from a tackle. Fifty-fifty balls were usually Ralph's.

He was built of moorland granite, stood over six feet tall and had thighs like milk churns. His thick, droopy moustache lent him an air of menace, although he was a quiet gentleman off the field. 'You'll come home one day with a broken leg,' his mother had said at half-time one Saturday when he was performing in a Herald Cup game. 'T'wont be mine, though, mother,' Ralph grinned.

During the bad winter of 1947 he got his van halfway up the Beacon before the snow won. Even then he delivered the post on foot despite the drifting and the blizzard raging across the Dartmoor in-country. He spent the next five days at the farm and helped the farmer feed the stock after the hay was dropped by RAF planes.

During the same arctic winter Ralph's Post Office van saw the birth of Mrs Tozer's son, Henry, during a mercy mission that ended in the drifts of Long Lane. Ralph and Mr Tozer delivered the baby.

Throughout the Great Ammil of '47 Ralph brought wood and food to pensioners cut off by the snow and was out with the other men to collect provisions dropped in the fields by the RAF.

He would have liked to have led the village team to the Herald Cup Final but that honour escaped him. Recently his wife died but he lives on in the cottage by the pub, an active old man still in possession of his health and his hair. He is secretary of the village football club and whenever I shoot my mouth off during a match or am guilty of a bad tackle old Ralph grins at me and wags a finger and says: 'Get home do, boy, – at your age! At your age! If you didn ougher know better who did?'

The Church House, Stoke Gabriel, South Devon

Once in a while I walk or cycle out to Stoke Gabriel and end up at the Church House Inn.

Swinging along I'm usually mugged by nostalgia and let the past come alive. My old man marched me through these lanes when I was a tacker with a taste for sweet cider and an appetite for rural Britain which remains healthy four decades later.

Dad had his favourite watering holes along his Sunday Walks where he would top up on scrumpy or best bitter depending on the weight of the loose change in his pocket.

The Church House Inn was one of those happy places at the end of the Yellow Brick Road where the Apple People gathered to test the quality of the pressings from local orchards.

Here, my old man could 'romance' among celebrated 'romancers', spinning his amazing yarn which became more convoluted as his cider intake rose and the colour rose in his cheeks and nose.

The Church House hasn't really changed a lot over the years. The lounge bar has that Olde Worlde atmosphere fed by the big fireplace, the salmon fishermen and assorted boat people.

The bell ringers gather in their corner to discuss whatever bell ringers discuss while the euchre players gather in the tiny snug of a public beneath the muzz of local dialect. I sometimes join them with Dave Baker to reacquaint myself with the mysteries of benny and bower.

Spring is a good time to visit the Church House. Then it is satisfactory to sit on the bench outside and listen to the swifts screaming and the pigeons crooning as the Agricultural Wine gently unscrews your kneecaps.

The Bradfords provide traditional pub grub and I always enjoy meeting the old boys over a lunchtime noggin.

But more often than not the May sunshine and the Devon accent resurrect my father's ghost and he's there in his best Co-op off-the-peg suit delivering my half of sweet cider on another spring noon time has blurred.

CHAPTER THREE

Village Walkabout

Ashprington

The best way to visit Ashprington is to walk from Totnes along the public footpath that leaves the town about 50 yards up the hill from The Steam Packet Inn. It's a route that runs high above the River Dart, through woods and fields, until you glimpse the tower of Ashprington Church over the tree tops and come down the lane into the village.

The walk is short, the views memorable, the going easy; and at the end your reward is a neat little collection of predominantly grey stone buildings standing under slate roofs in gardens muzzed with the drone of bees.

Ashprington is 'picturesque' without the cloying prettiness

Village Characters No. 1 The Farmer.
Mr Albert Rogers of Coombe
Farm, Ashprington, Devon

of some of those Walt Disney villages which feature on the worst country calendars. It's good on the eye.

I used to come here backalong after picking strawberries on a nearby farm. Then it was fine to swill beer in the Durant Arms and wash away the taste of the fruit. Late the other morning I strolled in to be greeted by flower scent and birdsong.

Big summer clouds drifted across the South Hams and the swifts were flying high. Ashprington belongs to the retired and newcomers who really care about the environment, but my dad would have lamented the absence of the Devon accent and the closure of the school, which is now a private house.

For me the village school always registers as the heart of the community, a place where its tomorrows are shaped. The institution must be preserved at all cost and the Government should learn to think small again in the rural context.

I took the lane opposite Askew Cottage and wandered past a modern grey stone building which time will weather, and came on to Red Hill Cottage. A pair of wellies stood in the porch. Boots on a doorstep, like smoke from a chimney, tell you a house has blood in its stones. It is lived in.

I admired the ceramic name plaque fixed to the wall of Holly Villas that weren't villas but handsome cottages with carved wooden gables. Further on, a white cat with black ears and a black tail sat under the hedge being scolded by a thrush.

Behind the hedge was the village cemetery but I swung away to the right into another of Ashprington's delightful backwaters to find more grey stone cottages and an amazing old outside lavatory. The grey stone was the sort of honeyed colour you find in nature. 'Number 7 and 8 Holly Villas' was printed elegantly on the inevitable ceramic plaque. Here I met little Kate and Lydia Frater and their Shetland pony, Perky.

The blend of past and present was harmonious, and old farm buildings had been incorporated into the latest development. I liked the weather-tiled wall of the house standing near some unobtrusive bungalows which were set in big well-kept gardens behind tall hedges. A couple of village elders gossiped in one of the best vegetable plots I've ever seen with its rows of beans and other produce.

Leaning on the garden wall I could stare through my

thoughts at the church while the washing gently flapped on the clothes lines and the swallows shrilled and the sun beat down on the rooftops.

Among the older cottages were a handful of discreet up-market properties and plenty of gardens to soften the collision of the ancient and modern. Orchard Cottages were stone and slate; the walls of Twin Cottages had been given a pastel wash; the larger, grander white and black Coach House had a flight of three stone steps which folk once ascended to mount their horses.

I consulted my watch. It was the time of day when a man may sink a pint without reproaching himself, but first I had to look at the War Memorial. The granite cross inscribed with the names of the local dead of two world wars is the common bond of nearly all British villages.

Over the road was the Durant Arms, an 18th Century inn where I was pleasantly surprised by the draught Murphy's Irish Stout.

The walls of the lower bar were covered with olde worlde farm implements — scythes, pitch-forks, saws as well as coloured prints of hunting scenes. Next to the stag's antlers near the door was a large, glittering mid-Atlantic machine for space invader fans. I went through the beer garden into the other bar which was as comfortable as my mum's back room.

Outside, the sparrow nestlings up in the eaves were lisping. A car cornered and cruised downhill towards Bow Creek, and I followed at a more leisurely pace. On the left were Rose Cottages and their sun-soaked grey stone. Every village has its Rose Cottages but the ceramic name plaque which cropped up again was beginning to intrigue me. And these buildings could boast small windows and lovely rectangular porches which might inspire American tourists to soar into hyperbole.

Further on a choir of fowls scratched for worms in a few square yards of soil. Their contented clucking brought child-hood summers alive. A tractor passed at speed. I paused at a wooden building which proved to be the Village Hall although it looked like a cricket pavilion. Then I walked on to Ashprington Post Office Stores and Off-Licence.

I confess to really loving these tiny shops. They have bags of character as well as a bit of everything. In the window was a poster advertising a 'Russian Summer Party at Sandwell

Manor' with 'Folk Dances of Eastern Europe and Russia', and 'Dancing to Wild Borscht'.

Inside I browsed among the fruit and veg, the tins, bottles and packets by the pale glow of the freezer while the proprietors, Mr and Mrs Gooderham, served their customers. The things a village can't do without, from toilet rolls to Scotch, were on display and here I solved the mystery of the ceramic plaques. The door bell tinkled and a young lady appeared carrying a load of brown paper parcels. She was Susan Farrell, of Tuckenhay, whose pottery house names and numbers were so popular locally.

For me a village store can resurrect the past both vividly and poignantly. In the sunshine again I caught the shrilling of the swallows and the banjo music of the hens. All it needed to complete the moment was my gran coming up the road with her shopping basket on her arm.

A cock crowed and I sauntered down to Coombe Farm. Sheep lay under the apple trees in the orchard above the outbuildings and the healthy stink of animal manure hung over the place.

Mr Albert Rogers' half weather-tiled farmhouse was a gem of South Hams architecture. It had splendid ornate green eaves and the sort of undefiled exterior that lifts the heart. Mr Rogers was digging his vegetable garden. He was a cheerful 66-year-old Devonian from Cornworthy with a mop of white hair. His family had moved to Coombe Farm in 1940.

Together we bemoaned the exodus of youngsters from the community, but few newly-weds can afford a house priced around the £70,000 mark. The solution to the problem eluded us, but I was happy to have met a man with red soil in his voice, someone who still looked to his roots and cared about the future of his kind.

The road beyond Coombe was narrow. It ran beneath an enormous lime tree, past Lime Tree Cottage to Frogmore Farm, the last building in that part of Ashprington. I retraced my steps to the wooden bus shelter, the telephone box and village notice board, all of which were near the War Memorial. Turning left I met Mrs Shirley Millman outside her cottage, Cherrytrees. She was Ashprington born and bred and I was glad to hear my own accent yet again on someone else's lips. But I was saddened when she informed me that only half a dozen native villagers remained.

Across the way the Old Rectory was now a nursing home. I glanced up at the chestnut tree recalling a windy autumn evening many years ago and a gang of kids knocking down the conkers. Then I walked up to the church with yesterday fading behind my eyes. Cloud was piling up in the north. Maybe it would thunder but the swallows were still flying high so I wasn't worried.

At the church I climbed the steps to the lych gate and stepped into a graveyard that was full of tall, seeding grasses and moon daisies. From here it was possible to take in Ashprington's compactness.

I could look east across the roofs to a tilting field full of cattle and south into a vision of the South Hams. On the lawn at the back of Cherrytrees immediately below me the Millman's crinkled white dog was dozing. Several mallard ducks and drakes slept on the gravestones and washing hung on lines in gardens which met the surrounding farmland without fuss.

Meanwhile, down on the duck pond of Ashprington Court Farm the more energetic mallard were afloat. It was one of those pastoral cameos you dream about when you're abroad and bored. Ashprington Church fed my mood. It is one of the few churches dedicated to the patron saint of Wales, St David. The sandstone tower had weathered to perfection and the porch was very high and had swallows' nests in three of its ceiling corners.

The notice pinned to the door carried instructions printed in a child's hand 'Enter quietly and shut the door. The birds nesting above will come in, make a mess and die.' I obeyed.

A Celtic chapel once stood on the site of this medieval parish church. Perhaps the saint himself rested here on his travels from Wales in the 6th century and founded the place. Bow Creek was less than a mile away and those Celtic Christians favoured sheltered inlets on the tidal rivers of Devon.

Speculation apart, the interior's smallness, austerity and lack of Victorian gloom were reminders of its distant origins. I admired the Norman font and the modern carving on the pulpit and dropped some coins in the wall box before departing.

The leaves of the oak by Church Cottages were whispering. I stood under the tree and the cat with the black ears and black tail threaded in and out of my legs. Against the clouds the swifts flickered over Ashprington and I turned and walked up the sun-dappled lane.

Halcyon days at Denbury

I like arriving in the village on foot with an appetite for everything the place has to offer and a respectable beer thirst.

That morning the weather was mild and unseasonable but the sun was out after a week of grey skies. I came past the Union Inn, and the village green with the high stone wall of Denbury Manor on my right.

A little further on was on imposing stone arch and a lodge house. The gates were open, offering a peep into that world of gracious county living you rarely experience outside the pages of *Country Life*. A crow said caw! and I walked up South Street with the past gradually assembling under slate roofs.

Denbury's cottage architecture conjured up memories of the marvellous summer holidays of my childhood when I cycled to these places. There was Honeysuckle Cottage with its honeysuckle, and Number 14 South Street with its pointed arch and pink-washed walls. Penwith and Minstrel Cottages crouched under the low, blunt tower of Denbury Church.

Swallows dipped between buildings as I came to the centre of the village where four roads met – North, South, East and West Streets. The hub of the crossroads was the War Memorial and here I found a covey of Devonshire folk. Ruby Beaty, who was born in Harbertonford, was chatting to Annie Lang whose great grandparents had worked Peartree Farm. These gracious old ladies were joined by Sid Ellis, another vintage villager and native of Denbury. Mr Ellis was the captain of the bell ringers and looked after the churchyard.

Mrs Lang told me about the animals' drinking trough which had stood beside the War Memorial, and how each street once had its own tap for the householders. Her neighbour, Mrs Tate, smiled and nodded. She had kept the village Post Office Stores in the halcyon days of wooden counters and glass fronts, and I considered the changes which had devastated parts of Torbay.

I'm glad Denbury is still rich in the past. This respect for yesterday lends many of our villages dignity and repose. Mrs

Lang showed me Number 5 East Street, the oldest house in Denbury.

'It's got a wooden staircase,' she said, and I admired the tall, fat chimneys and the absence of the twee.

Then I walked with Mrs Lang to the churchyard and we watched Mr Ellis cutting the grass.

'My great grandfather's buried over there,' she said, pointing. 'He was 84.' And she chuckled and added: 'His four wives are buried under him. As they died off he went and got himself a new one.'

The Church of St Mary the Virgin had an attractive little graveyard. Among the headstones was a stone statue of a Boy Scout. The tower boasted a blue, diamond-shaped clock face with gold hands and numerals. The interior of the church was long, narrow and medieval. It had been built to accommodate the spiritual needs of a small community. The ceiling was curved and white and there was an organ loft behind the pink sandstone font. Maybe Annie Lang's great gran'dad had stared about himself as I did while he sat contemplating his next wedding all those years ago.

The church dates from the 13th century, and the guide pamphlet informed me that 'unlike most Devon Churches it was cruciform in shape with transepts but no side aisles'. It also possessed that faint musty smell which I associate with the sabbath because it reminds me of Sunday services endured when I was the most reluctant of choirboys.

I went out into the westerly wind to find the trees rocking and sunlight scattering as it does in the spring. Even the great yew with its bole of immense girth was finding it difficult to handle the gale. Sid Ellis smiled at me and sent his mowing machine clattering through the grass. I strolled up East Street past Mrs Lang's home and the Old School House and some magnificent cottages. New development was out of sight up the road and I didn't go in search of it.

Returning to the War Memorial I paused at the top of West Street to photograph the Old Village Shop which is now closed and neglected. West Street had its share of lovely historic cottages. I wandered past Denbury Garage and saw the new grey stone school building and heard the noise coming from the kitchen windows as lunch was prepared.

Few things warm the heart like the sight of a living village

Village chaRacteRs No. 2
The ButcheR
Eddie Langworthy of NoRth
StReet, DenbuRy.

school and the sound of treble voices shrilling with all the promise of the future. I glanced up at Denbury Down, the site of a battle between Roundheads and Cavaliers. Ahead was more new housing so I walked back to the Memorial and had another chat with the ladies before setting off along North Street. Here Haytor House made me look down the road to a distant horizon of Dartmoor and Hay Tor prominent in the bottom of the sky. Then I discovered Eddie Langworthy's butcher shop with its floor of Denbury marble and the man himself behind the counter wrapping up a pound of his famous hand-mixed sausages.

The place was small but the horns taken from a highland bull and displayed on the partition were huge. Eddie was one of those happy, outgoing Devonians who make a mockery of the West Country rural stereotype you meet in daft TV fiction.

'If you kin see Hay Tor it's goin' to rain,' he grinned. A Bickington boy, he had been in the business for half a century – on pushbike and in the van and with his mobile. There was a constant coming and going of customers and a lot of friendly banter. Before I left he gave me some of his sausages and said, with a wink: 'Don't forget, I take American Express.'

Not far from Eddie's was the Post Office Stores flanked by pleasant cottages. Inside were stacked the usual village essentials, and the proprietor, Mr Wood, was handing out the sort of personal service you expect to get in these timeless little establishments.

Stepping into the street again I saw Hay Tor masked in rain and wondered if we were going to get another depressing summer. But the cottages and their low porches cheered me up and the walking brought me to the gate of North End Farm.

Big fit free range fowls were scampering about the yard with a gusto that sprang from outdoor life, and while I was watching them Mrs Margaret Wakeham emerged from her farmhouse. She proved to be another cheerful soul in her wellies and glasses – Devon to the core like Eddie, and full of good humour. Her husband farmed elsewhere and she looked after North End with its ten acres, one cow, two calves and the chickens.

Beyond her place Denbury met the fields with a modest flourish of bungalows which persuaded me to turn around and head for the village green and the pub. The green was spacious. On occasions it was the setting for Morris dancing and clog dancing and other happenings which many believe necessary to the village soul.

Over 400 years of history had been invested in the Union Inn, and South Devonians will perhaps recall it in the era of Harry Lark, 53 years its landlord. Roy and Gill Smart supply today's good cheer. Roy was a North Sea diver who gave up walking the sea bed to keep an inn and perform with the Newton Bushel Morris Men. Thursday evenings in his pub are devoted to live music from folk groups like Skiddy Whidden.

At the bar I met my old soccer buddy, Mike Curtis, who shares my passion for the game and can't wait to put on his boots for any charity match that's going. We spoke of the 'good old days' in the South Devon League because they were good and football took us to nearly every village from Prawle Point to Chagford.

And we agreed that whatever communities like Denbury have to offer – Eddie's sausages, Mrs Lang's snippets of local history, Margaret Wakeham's cheerfulness, the church, the shop, the cottages and the inn – you'll also come away with a heavy dose of nostalgia.

Stoke Gabriel

I walked past the Old Forge into a leafy lane away from the cars and Port Bridge. The weather forecast had got it wrong and the sun shone between clouds, winking and flashing through the foliage.

Soon Byter Mill was behind me and I was climbing the hill to walk above Mill Pool with Californian-type bungalows on my right.

The Pool revived childhood memories. As a boy I would wander out of my home town of Paignton into another world. Here generations of Stoke Gabriel kids have learnt to swim and the creek is full of the little phantoms of lost forever summers.

The lane brought me deeper into the Sunday morning and the sound of church bells. That music can send me drifting back over the years to other sabbaths and walks taken with my dad. The village has grown since then and some of the development lacks imagination but for all that Stoke remains one of the Dart's most pleasant communities.

I strolled up the narrows of Coombe Shute, past pink and

Village Characters No.3 Everyone's Friend
Aunt Jess of The Barnhay,
Stoke Gabriel, Devon.

white cottages, to gaze over the slate roofs and apple trees at the tower of St Mary's and St Gabriel's Church. The lane dropped down in front of the Victoria and Albert, the friendly pub set among attractive houses.

I sauntered on up the hill to the Church House Inn which I first visited in the 1940s when my dad started my scrumpy apprenticeship. The pub was one of his occasional weekend 'watering holes'.

Later, when I had mastered the craft of sinking pints of farmhouse rough, I came here to sit outside reading and relaxing in the evening sun. That was during the reign of Marshall and Blanche Baker.

The inn was an eccentric-looking white building with black paintwork, a porch and a penthouse roof over the lower windows. Bits and pieces had been added to the place throughout its history. It is at least 850 years old and is prospering under the landlordship of Geoff Bradford and his wife, Margaret. I come there for the Devon accent and euchre in the snug. I like to sit at the table with my old mate Dave Baker and take on Doris the barmaid and Barry. Euchre is the most Celtic of card games, with Benny and Bowers and the bewilderment it can rouse in the uninitiated. I play with all the refinement and restraint of a kamikazi pilot and tolerant locals draw straws to see who will be unfortunate enough to get me for a partner!

The Church House Inn of River Dart chat, seine netters on the beer after an evening on the water, members of the church choir in their corner of the lounge, the fire roaring up the chimney in the winter, newcomers and natives mingling, holidaymakers soaking up the 24-carat West Country atmosphere!

The pub was closed and the Bradfords' dogs Lassie and Ben were snoozing on the front doorsteps. I turned right, past Stoke Gabriel Post Office, the Devon Shop and Orchard Stores where you can buy good home-cured hams. The big houses and bungalows lining the road had a Thirties air about them but Townwell, with its green door and porch, pink wash and rose-hung walls, was one of those rare buildings of beauty and character which would enhance any village.

A little further on Gabriel Court provided a tantalising glimpse of yew topiary arches and a sweep of vegetable gardens. The white tower of the hotel, crowned with a tiled 'steeple', was more seaside than rural. Sir John Betjeman would have celebrated its uniqueness in verse.

Leaving the War Memorial I loped on up the hill. Big houses in big gardens were half-hidden above me on the right. A lot of building was still in progress but beyond Lotus Pottery and the converted byres and barns was Yarde – a handsome white-washed house belonging entirely to an age which created things to last. I had entered one of those timeless reaches which the sound of the hover mower couldn't disturb. The church bells continued to provide perfect mood music.

Hunched beneath tottering chimneys was an ancient grey cottage and nearby King's Cottage held its small windows to the sun. Meanwhile, valerian nodded from wayside walls and daws were jangling above the roofs. I could look down over the wall to my left into the kitchen windows of a row of pink cottages.

On the opposite side of the road were some really expensive properties discreetly placed behind shrubberies and trees. Past and present met with considerable astonishment but I wish Old Orchard was still Maddick's Orchard, with its cider apple trees instead of the new Wimpey homes.

Maybe I might have gone on up the road past Stoke Gabriel Baptist Church and chapel to have a look at Rydon Acres if the stray dog hadn't trotted past me in the other direction. Rydon Acres is a spacious housing estate immured in calm privacy but the dog seemed to be setting off on an adventure, so I followed it.

Instead of a green Stoke had an orchard in the centre of the village. I remembered Alf Tucker bagging fruit under the trees for the cider-making backalong. Rooks cawed, a car cruised by and the bells stopped ringing. The road took a sharp left hand turn into School Hill with School Hill Cottages prominent and history rearing its cheerful head again.

The trees each side of Duncannan Lane made one of those 'tunnels of green gloom' poets rave about but I resisted its lure and strode down past the village hall to the school. Few village schools have the charm of Stoke Gabriel primary. There was a lawn and a Maypole, flowers and apple trees in the front garden. Roses climbed the walls. It was a 'Larkrise to Candleford' place, very summery, generating a wonderful optimism.

At the Paper Shop I headed down Mill Hill after the signpost had told me that was the way to the River Dart. On the corner Mill Hill Cottage was waiting to bring a smile of pleasure to the face of anyone addicted to old thatched dwellings. It stood next to Mill Hill Court and the sort of suburban development that excites estate agents.

Soon I was beside Mill Pool. Cars were parked along the bank and people were sun-bathing in deckchairs. From the dam and quay I could look across the Dart to the far bank. To my right were old houses bearing explicit names like 'Tides Reach'.

Things change but the seine netting of salmon hasn't altered greatly over the decades. The season runs from 15 March to 16 August and crews of four take to their boats on various stretches of the Dart. In the old days the net was 'shot' so that it spread and sank quickly. Now it is rolled out of the stern, and hauled from the land in the time honoured way.

Whenever I think of seine netting, old Stoke Gabriel families come to mind: the Baker clan, the Hills and the Collinses.

Each of the 18 seine net boats on the Dart has its own water. Ten boats operate from Stoke Gabriel in a business that is governed by the tides. The biggest salmon taken on the river was caught in 1914 by Captain Rowe. It weighed 50½lbs and a photo of the fish can be seen in the Church House Inn. Captain Rowe was Blanche Baker's father.

Walking back to browse around the churchyard I turned into one of Stoke's secret blackwaters – The Barnhay. Here I found myself wandering into a narrow alley between small country gardens. Eighty-two-year-old 'Aunt' Jess Collings was talking to three young girls outside Rose Cottage and as I bent to stroke a dusty black cat I was joined by Doris, the barmaid from the Church House. She showed me 'Aunt' Pat's Lane where a lot of village lads and lassies have done their courting. Aunt Pat lived in Gate House and served teas in her garden next to the churchyard, mainly for cadets from the Royal Naval College at Dartmouth.

We strolled back to Mill Hill and came around by the popular Castle pub and The Butchery for a look at the Church House Inn from another angle. Several visitors were outside the pub waiting for the doors to open. Doris went inside and I walked on to the church past another row of cottages and the Old School.

Alas, the Home Guard hut where the village soccer teams changed for years had gone. Names from the football club's past surfaced as I hesitated at the Lych Gate – the Hills and Hingstons, Moysey, Baker, Hammy Collings. Hammy was a hell of a character, a stocky bloke with the power of an ox in his shoulder charge, a legend who never pulled out of the tackle.

Those days are gone now, although Stoke's most fiery supporter, Pam Emmins, is alive and kicking. She gave me stick whether I was playing for the village or turning out for the opposition.

I entered the churchyard and was greeted by the faint sound of the organ and hymn-singing from within the building. The stubby red sandstone tower stood against the clouds. Beneath it was an enormous old yew tree and its spread of boughs pressed down among the graves. Leaving the shade I found the sun and a marvellous quietude overlooking Mill Pool. Then I came and stood before the headstones which marked the resting places of Ivor Andrews and 'Nip' Hannaford Hill, who were drowned in the Dart in one of those tragedies which visit riverside communities century after century. I used to play euchre with Nip in what was then the Council Club in Paignton.

All around me Stoke Gabriel's past was asleep but not forgotten. The churchyard was full of wild flowers. In the creek the tide was turning, a heron flopped down on the far shore, shelduck flighted in, a child laughed and a blackbird began to sing.

Coffinswell

It was drizzling but walking in from the Newton Abbot direction I was met by the cheerful sight of Coffinswell's thatch. Rock Cottage and its companion even had thatched roofs on the porches and enough roses to drive several hives of bees crazy with joy.

While I was admiring them a lean, loose-limbed Siamese cat jogged across the road and pleaded for attention. I carried it back to the lawn of 'Rustlings' and left it cleaning itself.

The country road ran past elegant homes which were almost

Village Characters No 4
The Retired Water Board man
Eddie Skinner of Coffinswell, Devon.

lost in their large, tidy grounds. On the other side a stream gurgled through the more modest garden of Dodswell Cottage, but I wandered by some contemporary dwellings to a cottage that was not only thatched but also had a woodpile and loads of what certain glossy magazines call 'rustic charm'. Further up the hill was Alma Cottage and its porch with a pointed, tiled roof.

The mixture of old and new houses in gardens which made me both happy and envious accounted for much of Coffinswell's appeal. It was a small village as most children imagine villages to be and it lay under acres of thatch. Keeping an eye open for idiosyncracies I found one in the shape of a mini-cattle grid in the entrance to the garden of Fairway Cottage.

'Cottage' was the operative word. There was Old Manor Cottage wearing old thatch, and above it were a handful of grey stone outbuildings with ivy-clad walls and rusty corrugated roofs. The hillside behind was covered in small fields and trees.

Moments later I reached the Manor House and its gardens and shrubberies. Lots of summer-leafing trees concealed whatever lay to the left of the road. I liked the Manor House. It had fig trees and old byres which smelt pleasantly of animal living. Despite the drizzle swallows were hawking insects above the rooftops and twittering as they worked.

At the bend and a homestead named Cherang Tuli a sidelane dipped to the right and presented yet another of those glimpses of thatch which I couldn't resist. There were inconspicuous bungalows and more of yesterday's cottages and the countryside waiting beyond the last garden to carry you out of yourself into Nature.

Walking up the hill again to Cherang Tuli I saw the tall chimneys and prominent red brick facade of a very grand house to the left in the distance. But the road had its own architectural delights and coming down it towards me were young Kathryn Palfreman and Claire Bedell exercising a brace of dogs apiece for Ashlands Kennel.

The drizzle had stopped and it became so warm I thought the sun was about to break through. The girls gave me a 'good morning' and I pointed my camera at a white cottage before turning to the row of superb pink-washed cottages. They really were gems, and where they ended I discovered a mock-Tudor eccentricity with a half-timbered upper storey on two stone pillars and a red section.

It probably dated from the turn of the century and had been the lodge of the Old Rectory which hadn't been the rectory at all, just a place called Home Fields. Staring across the landscaped gardens I was confronted by the big red brick house I had first seen from the lane below Cherang Tuli. I suppose it had been someone's idea of living in style, a country seat. Well, *Ut umbra, sic vita.*

On the next bend Appledore Cottage and its thatch, roses and resident sparrows was everyone's dream of 'getting away from it all' fulfilled. I strolled on, whistling 'Greensleeves', into the heart of cottageland: Court Barn Cottage, Willa Cottage and Court Barton Cottage looking a bit different under a slate roof.

Below the Milber Road were Princess Cottages, a row of solid dwellings which also had tiled roofs. In the garden of Number 5 I met Mrs Peggy Baker tending her flowers. She proved to be a quiet-spoken Devonian who loved the village. After telling me the Jack Russell that came sniffing round my ankles was called Skippy she introduced me to Mr Eddie Skinner, her neighbour from Number 6. He was a Combe-inteignhead man. Retired from the Water Board he had lived in Coffinswell for 45 years.

It isn't chauvinism that makes me respond so warmly to the Devon accent. Villagers like Peggy Baker and Ed Skinner remind me of my grandparents and my dad. The language was butter on my father's tongue. For him stew was 'stoo' and a dog, a 'dug' and bramble, 'brimble'. Maybe these village walkabouts are part of a quest for my pastoral origins as well as the need to nourish my roots. And I love the regional accents which I've sought from the Hebrides to Lands End since I was young.

Mr Wills of Manor Farm went by on his tractor with a muddy sheepdog up behind him and I let my legs carry me to The Linny, the village free-house and restaurant. It was thatched, homely and 14th century. But 14th century what, I wondered, as George Sykes showed me around his bar. The linhays which had been converted not so long ago probably dated from that period. Now George and his wife Ann have the sort of country pub many licensees would give their back teeth to run.

I regretted it wasn't opening time as I ambled off to the church. Leaving the village limits I found a black iron gate and a footpath which led to the churchyard. The absence of trees left 'Gods Acre' open to whatever light the overcast morning could muster. Alas, the Church of St Bartholomew was locked although the tower was open and I could sneak a look at the certificates the bellringers had won at various ringing festivals.

Mooching around the outside of the building I stoked up quite a hatred for the vandals who force church authorities to lock the doors. Vandalism appears to be a problem mainly encountered near large towns and cities. The pervading sadness of St Bartholomew's may have owed something to the depressing weather but it reached into Court Barton Farm next door.

St Bartholomew's has some claim to fame for there can't be many churches which are served by a path running through a farmyard. Yet Court Barton looked ready to give up the ghost. The beautiful 14th or 15th century farmhouse that was right out of the novel *Tom Jones* needed attention.

The cobbled yard and exquisite stone entrance arch were also decaying. Then across the cobbles came a dark, almost black, Sumatra game hen and her chicks watched by two workdogs and a Sumatra cockerel that trailed lavish tail feathers. His 'train' shimmered blue and green. Life could still stride confidently out of corners of neglect.

I returned to the Linny hoping Coffinswell would never be subjected to insensitive development. Like so many of our villages, as it stands it is a national asset.

Harbertonford

Old Harbertonford was built from stone fetched in horse-drawn wagons from the quarry at Rolster Bridge further up the River Harbourne.

But I was on Steve Jane's lawn in front of his bungalow watching the traffic swish by in an endless parade, up and down the Totnes Road.

The bungalow was called 'Up Yonder' and stood near what was once the police house in Mill Meadow.

Across the way the grey steeple of St Peter's Church was proving irresistible to the swifts.

Along the road was a little modern development which

Village Characters No 5
The Champion Gardener
Eddie White of Harbertonford,
Devon.

wouldn't offend the builders of the past who seemed to have worked in harmony with the landscape.

It was a sunny morning. All around the village small hills glided up into a blue, cloudless sky.

'Harbertonford's still a working village,' Steve told me. 'Not so long ago practically every man was employed at the woollen mill or on the land.'

Steve is a bricklayer-mason with the South Hams District Council.

He is also Harbertonford FC. After the original 'Ford Football Club folded in 1949 Charlie Priddle got it going again in 1955. Steve was a player who became Secretary in 1960 and at 54 anticipates seeing the club into the next century.

Steve and his wife Val, who was a Treeby, have two sons and are actively involved in village life. Val's dad introduced electricity to Harbertonford from a small generator. I like that. It's an essentially British achievement, a bit of scaled-down rural enterprise.

'What makes me sad,' Steve said as we walked the road towards The Maltsters, 'is we've no village bobby. Every community ought to have its policeman.'

Although born in East Allington the man spoke of Harbertonford with pride, and he gave me some of the names of the old village families – the Homes, Whites, Shinners, Treebys and Hannafords.

The rooks in the tall trees of the copse beyond the church kicked up a racket. Swifts screamed. The traffic roared by, nose to tail, ferrying sun worshippers to the beaches of the South Hams.

We came to the Old School House standing next to the Old School. Both buildings were Victorian masterpieces in weathered grey slate stone. The school house had ornate wooden gables and fine windows with granite cornices; the school could offer an 'Alice in Wonderland' clock and rock gardens full of flowers to heighten the summery mood.

A stream clattered under the roses and vanished by Brewery Cottages which were also a nice little chunk of the past.

Alan Bennett and his wife, Shirley, who created the old school garden, came out to talk about the building and the village.

A labrador passed with a gentleman in tow, and Mrs Lister

and friends lingered to peer, perhaps into their own yesterdays.

During the war, dances were held in the school and conjuring up a vision of the scene made me also think of the occupation of much of the South Hams by American servicemen.

Swifts hurtled over the rooftops but we were content to dodge the traffic and saunter through the churchyard.

St Peter's, Harbertonford, is the classic Victorian notion of the medieval made reality. There were flowers in the porch and the nave was clean and attractive with a well-cared-for atmosphere set off by the timber roof and the stained glass windows behind the altar.

Leaving the church and its grassy graveyard we went through a side gate into Woodland Road which is still known to locals as Factory Road.

Who changes the old place names in villages, and why?

I was confronted by a row of cottages wearing plain washes from dark bottle green to white. Their eaves were clotted with sparrows and between some of the buildings were stone corridors which I've always called 'drangs'.

We went through one of these into vegetable gardens that ran for about 30 yards down to the lovely tree-fringed River Harbourne.

At the back of his home I met 59-year-old Mr Bonzo Beer and his wife Pru. Bonzo had retired after working at the woollen mill where things like Naval serge, blankets and horse bandages were once made.

The old mill had been two storeys higher in the Forties and Fifties but the demolition experts have accounted for that particular piece of the past and the 125-foot chimney stack.

Bonzo was a cheerful man entirely at ease in the succulent jungle of his vegetables. Steve and I walked on past the modern development of Church Court with the copse and rookery on our right. Banks of foxgloves climbed to the trees. The Englishness of it all brought a smile to my face.

'That's Mill Court,' Steve said, pointing to the pleasant white house on the other side of the road. 'The foundation bricks came from the mill stack. The Palmers love it there.'

Understandably, I thought, with the rooks up above in the front and the Harbourne at the bottom of the garden.

Raking over our soccer yesterdays we returned to the main road and The Maltsters, a pub in the old tradition of village pubs. The landlord, Paul Scoble and his wife Pat, are Devonian and their place is alive with all the warmth of the community. Pat was washing down her front doorstep when we tip-toed over the wet stone into the bar.

On one wall were old photographs of village activities and characters. The Scobles' three dogs, Cheeko, Pugsley and Mutley, slept on the floor. It was a comfortable snug of a pub with decorative bits of the farming past hanging from the walls — scythes and other implements which once spelt out the drudgery of agricultural life.

Shove ha'penny, darts and euchre struck me as the sort of social activities that go well with ale, cider and oggies.

In a hostelry like The Maltsters, faced by a black-and-white photo of the village team taken perhaps in the club's golden days, it would have been difficult not to boot about on Memory Meadow.

Harbertonford's pitch is one of Farmer Arthur Finch's fields — The Hams.

Steve spoke about Ralph Ryder, Mike Stumbles, Bob Richards, good old Jeff Palfrey and a regiment of local lads like Keith Hack, Les Steer, The Trants, Phil Edwards, and the Geordie-Devonian, Bob Monaghan.

Some of the young tearaways were sunning themselves across the other side of the Harbourne by the bridge. Three or four little girls were bathing in the river and a dog was splashing about just for the hell of it.

Then we met Mr Eddie White who had worked for 34 years at Stancombe Farm. Fifty years a show gardener, there wasn't much Eddie didn't know about vegetables. Maybe his grandson Mark who was with the old gentleman outside Harbertonford's Post Office Stores will be blessed with the sort of green fingers that win gold medals at championship shows.

Inside the stores, beyond the porch and the name of the building, Harbourne House, it was cool and surprisingly big. Tom and Christine Pring obviously had their fingers on the pulse of village requirements, from apples to alcohol and aspirin.

Opposite their place was The Hungry Horse, the popular restaurant which was once a row of four or five little cottages standing close to the river in an area notorious for flooding.

We ambled up the hill by Brewery Cottages and some more of the fabric of Harbertonford's history — Ford House that was once the village institute where you could eat fish and chips and play billiards (not, of course, at the same time!); Chapel Cottage, Peartree Court, Red Lion Cottage which had been a pub.

Stone buildings wore the pastel wash that I find so attractive. There was the Old Forge and the Old Bakery, whose names spoke for themselves and reached into my heart like a plea for the way things were.

In front of the cottages on the right with their upright slating was a little open gutter. Over the road flights of steps led into drangs and the one we entered suddenly became a lane creeping among old buildings, gardens, and outside lavs.

Two jackdaws sang out to each other on the roof of a linhay.

We walked the loop back towards the road between the walls of other ancient dwellings, including Court Cottage which was small and beautiful.

A left-hand turn and we were climbing the hill past the alcove where the village pump once stood next to Harbertonford Church of England Primary School. It was a modern brick building with lots of windows and it served several nearby communities as well as the village.

The playground was overlooked by copses, fields and orchards. Beyond the kid-sized goals of the kid-sized soccer pitch was a cow pasture. Then I was shown the open-air swimming pool and thought it would be fine for the children to be learning the breast stroke with Friesians mooing just over the way and the haymaking leaving parts of the hill opposite shorn and yellow.

I stared across the rooftops to the church steeple before turning to follow the flight of a kestrel down the wooded river valley towards Bow Creek.

Harbertonford's council estate was behind the trees to my left and in its splendid gardens above the school was Maryland House.

Walking slowly back to the bridge Steve talked about every aspect of village life.

'Mr Lovell Rogers has the farm at Brockhills,' he said as I tried to pick up a sinuous little black cat. 'And there's Farmer Atree of Hernaford up towards Halwell.' The cat wriggled from my grasp and shot up some steps.

Down on the bridge on The Maltsters side of the road some of the old boys were leaning against the parapet waiting for opening time, and I had to grin because I remembered my dad's Sunday morning rituals.

Harbertonford had plenty of Devon in its heart. Watching the river gliding by I didn't get that strong feeling of being a member of an endangered species which sometimes depresses me in Torbay.

Rattery

It was 6.15 am when I parked the car on what was once Rattery village green outside the Church House Inn.

Small birds were singing as I stepped out on to the tarmac and saw the sunlight falling across the front of the pub, illuminating some black lettering which told me the place dated back to AD 1028.

Jackdaws were taking off and landing but most villagers were still asleep. Beyond the rooftops and the daws was typical

Village Characters No. 6
The Retired Farm Worker
Fern Bovey of Rattery, Devon

South Devon countryside of fields, hedges, woods and little bumps of hills.

The smell of cow dung drifted across my thoughts and I wandered off like a poacher with the roads and lanes to myself.

Beyond the carpark, in the direction of South Brent, was a sign bearing the legend 'Allercombe Farm. The Barday Herd of British Friesians'.

An avenue of superb chestnut trees led down to Allercombe House where I was greeted by a charming pedigree kitten and a noble dwelling you'd expect to find in the 'Irish R.M.' TV series.

On the lawn was a gaudy posse of game fowl but I crept off before they could start squawking. It was too early to knock at the door and ask polite questions.

I returned to the road and found a dozen house martins sitting on the telephone wire. Maybe they couldn't wait to set off for Africa – the British summer being the usual token effort of a fortnight's seasonable weather.

The sunkissed byre of Glebe Farm was open to whatever the morning could manage. A red brick house stood among the jumble of outbuildings.

I yawned and retraced my steps and had a look around the churchyard that lay behind a pair of green wooden gates.

The Church of St Mary the Virgin waited on a hump that helped enhance its ecclesiastical stature. It rose from a crop of headstones to point the way to heaven. There was a weather-cock on top of the little steeple crowning the tower, and a fine granite arch provided the entrance to a porch of decorated plaster in faded pastel shades.

I tried the door and found it locked although the notice pinned to it read: 'Visitors welcome – God bless you.'

I strolled around the outside of the building and didn't find the grey-brown rendering at all ugly. It's funny how death never seems so grim in village churchyards. From the grass between graves I could look down on the blend of past and present.

Some of the modern development wasn't harmonious but the swifts hurtling by were the link between this age and yesterday. The past may devour us as individuals but life goes on and on.

I left the churchyard and made my way to Rattery Post

Office Stores which is run by Mrs Jenny Gurnall, a friendly lady who provides the Daz, meat pies, Twix, milk and spuds with genuine warmth. Her shop was closed. I frowned at my watch as I walked on. Sane people, I reflected, were snug abed.

A cock crowed and sunlight continued to spread across roofs and treetops.

Moments later I discovered a collection of small 'chalet' bungalows in a courtyard and a more satisfying row of what looked like good solid council houses nearby.

Careless architecture can disfigure a village and throughout my travels I've found a lot the planner has to answer for. But often the blame for the incongruous must be laid at the feet of central government which overrules parish councils and gives the go-ahead to the developer.

The village hall had plenty of character and so did Craven Cottage with its little windows, white walls and black shutters. I had come upon a beautiful flower-scented corner of Rattery.

Montrose Cottage drew me into a cul-de-sac where I was confronted by the whitewashed stonework and yellow paint of Burnside.

But these were architectural hors d'oeuvres which served to heighten the glory of Corbett Cottage. This was a work of art in weathered thatch and warm grey stone. The eaves were generous and the porch thatched.

The gardens at either hand were deep in herbs and flowers.

The birdsong had been turned down to summer level and even the daws tip-toeing over Corbett's thatch were whispering. It was the sort of place St Francis might choose for bed and breakfast accommodation if he decided to visit South Devon.

My saunter brought me through the faint stink of tom cat past an incredible breeze block bungalow and a display of roses worthy of the Chelsea Flower Show, over a stone bridge and a child of a stream into a lane on the right.

A couple of robust stone cottages promised much but beyond them some gardens and a bungalow stood between me and lots of green countryside.

So I returned to the road and the eccentric charm of Vines – a little thatched cottage at the wayside. It had gnomes on the garden walls and a porch with a pointed roof.

This was a fairy-tale village dwelling saved from the twee by its lovely 'lived-in' look. Maybe the Honda motorbike outside helped. It was gesture that excluded Mr Pickwick and Co!

In the yard of the cottage next door I met Michael Swain who used to teach my daughter when she was at Paignton School. He seemed happy in his rural retreat with an amiable old dog, ponies and a lifestyle in harmony with the living world.

Around the corner Mr Fern Bovey, of Garden Close, was rebuilding the side of his vegetable garden which had collapsed after heavy rain. He was a 79-year-old retired general labourer who had turned his hand to most things from lorry driving to rabbit trapping and farmwork.

'I'm still pretty active,' he grinned, leaning for a moment on his shovel. 'Work never killed no one and we've never ate out of tins or packets.'

He shifted some heavy stones and said: 'I don't have to hurry. I got all the time in the world.' He and his wife Milly were the only two born-and-bred villagers left in Rattery.

The world changes. Village life changes and there are few real working villages in this part of the country. There is no continuity of tradition despite the myths. This is inevitable for you can't expect a village to exist merely as a museum catering for our own romantic notions.

Informed regard for such communities, however, is essential to arrest a decline that is another facet of the destruction of rural beauty.

I stuffed my hands in my pockets and followed the hill up under the trees. Laurel Cottage, West Mead Cottage and West Mead House were splendid but beyond them the morning suddenly darkened.

I had wandered into a high, leaf-vaulted tunnel of trees which brought me to the outskirts of Rattery and the sunlight again.

A broad drive swept the eye into a mini country suburbia of bungalows in big gardens overlooking 'nice' views. Fortunately there were just two buildings.

Later, driving back towards Huxham's Cross, I pulled into a gateway for a chat with Farmer Derek Woodley of Parkland Farm, and cruising on for home considered what the visit had given me.

Rattery was an example of the changing face of village life throughout the land, but it had a lot to offer in this age of noise and haste.

Village Characters No.7
'The lady over the Road'
Mrs Ida Davis of Broadhempston, Devon.

What price do you put on tranquillity?

Broadhempston

Once upon a time, I suppose, Broadhempston was the classic 'street village' – one of those ancient rural communities which were built along the edges of a road.

Now it is a straggling place with a church, two pubs, a shop, a couple of farms and a real life of its own.

You can still find nostalgia blooming among the wisteria that trails over grey stone walls. Here all the country things townees love are orchestrated by summer into the pastoral dream – cottages and roses, bird calls, a whiff of cattle dung, ye olde worlde inn and a churchyard pinched from Gray's *Elegy*. But Broadhempston is also a working village with a strong core of Devonian families and concerned newcomers.

Outside the Coppa Dolla Inn the sign read: 'Consider our Local Residents – Please Leave Quietly.' Some visitors forget that people actually make their lives in the 'flowery nook' under the thatch and the screaming swifts. The past may be dozing in the odd corner, but the present asserts itself with unhurried confidence.

Coppa Dolla isn't one of those awful Mid-Atlantic names dreamt up by a catch-penny entrepreneur. It's from the Old English Coppede Ealdre – 'the decapitated alder' and refers to the settlement that grew around the first farm.

The pub dates from 1762 and the current innkeepers, Kathy and John Hosea, have brewed a most friendly atmosphere in their bar by keeping an excellent pint and providing tasty food and the opportunity to enjoy traditional pub conversation.

But it was too early to be thinking of ale so I sauntered past a building that advertised its age on the wall: AD 1473. Further up the hill I turned into a cobbled lane which disclosed one of those architectural eccentricities I'm always looking for. Blacklers Cottage had a flight of stone steps ascending its side wall to a door where someone with less imagination would have settled for a bedroom window.

Back on the road the modern bungalows at either hand gave way to Honeysuckle Cottage which was getting a new thatched roof, a little white cottage standing contentedly under its old thatch, and Wychway Cottage that was a tribute to contemporary development.

Up round the bend to the right was stately Ashwick House and beyond its clean white facade a lot of heavy farm machinery and vehicles were assembled in the yard of Broadhempston Plant Hire. In the lane behind the yard the blue silo towers of Wottons Farm brought a touch of the Space Age to the village.

But 'the poetry of Earth' wouldn't be denied and I followed some sheep back down the road to Ashwick Farmhouse. The sheep were following a man on a tractor and a very old collie was following the sheep.

At the bungalow by Ashwick Farmhouse I met Mrs Field who told me the farm had been in her husband's family for a long time. She also said Broadhempston was changing and added: 'Lots of people come and go.'

So did the farm vehicles! Tractors and the occasional Land Rover appeared and vanished into gateways or side roads as I headed for the centre of the village.

Waiting beyond the Coppa Dolla were the sort of twin cul-de-sacs that property dealers drool over. Rose Cottage possessed a porch at the front and the back which members of amateur art societies love to capture in watercolours.

Like Hamleigh and Court Gate, the cottage had flowers at its feet and clinging to its walls. Fuchsias and roses were competing with the alyssum to solicit bees. Immediately opposite this Rupert Brooke cameo was Poacher's Cottage and a mass of blooming pot plants. I tried to imagine the poachers I knew as a kid living there among the extravagant floral display. I couldn't.

My walk continued and I discovered that Manor Farm wasn't a farm anymore – it was a guest house. Across the road was a row of tiny cottages. Applecot looked small enough and pretty enough to fit into a fairy tale. But appearances are deceptive and I recalled a barrel-chested, boozy shark fisherman who occupied something similar on the West Coast of Ireland.

No such character, I hasten to add, lives in Broadhempston, although I remember village soccer matches which were quite physical. A certain good-humoured lad, named Ken Field, took no prisoners when he was wearing a Broadhempston shirt! He played as hard as he worked and today he has Borough Farm.

Outside the Old Salem chapel I was joined by two young villagers – Lisa Lewthwaite and her infant daughter Jasmine, and Anna Beadel and her little girl, Amy. They pointed out that the chapel was now a theatre although it wasn't much bigger than a linhay. Apparently the Crack Collective performed there, giving village-scale shows and demonstrating the Great British genius for thinking small.

We strolled down the road together to Borough Farm and its orchard. Friendly geese waddled through the long grass to greet the children who probably spoke fluent Goose as well as lots of other languages adults forget in the process of growing up.

Lisa and Anna talked warmly about Broadhempston and what it had to offer families with youngsters. It was a refreshing new slant on village life. I hoped the new houses going up beyond the farm would also prove to be examples of a respect for Yesterday without compromising Today.

While the women and their pushchairs went off to the shop I called in on a house at Stoops Cross. At Roughlands, Jonathan and Anne Read make wooden rocking horses, both the stand-base and bow-base varieties. The horses come in three sizes:

Little Henry, Charles and Big William and they cost from £250 upwards. The name of the husband and wife firm is Horseplay!

Maybe if my dad had taken back two or three lorry loads of his empty beer bottles when I was a kid I would have had a rocking horse. I grinned and the black and white cat lolling against the wall in the sun grinned back at me. So I came through my dreams to Broadhempston Post Office Stores.

Above the door of the solid stone building was one of those Lyons tea signs that can bring nostalgia to the boil. Behind the counter were Keith and Marlene Beer, a couple of Devonians with a cheerful, no-nonsense manner and a shop full of those standard bits and pieces which villages rely on.

Here I bumped into another of the Field clan, the mother of Ken. She used to teach at Broadhempston Primary School and was the stuff good rural communities are made of – a blend of common sense, native wit and humour.

Marlene Beer's mother, 79-year-old Mrs Ida Davis, came from a similar mould. She was in her front garden at No.2 Church Hill Cottages just across the road.

I left Mrs Davis's garden and came by Moorview Cottages to the village school which had just enough pupils to ensure its survival in our cockeyed educational system.

I strolled past the small grey building and had a look at the pub next door. The Monks Retreat turned out to be a 15th century inn offering real ale, farm cider and oak panelling.

I had to go under part of the pub to get into the churchyard at St Peter and St Paul. A sign at the entrance told naughty kids there was to be 'No Cycling or Skating'.

It was a grey church, standing to attention among the headstones. Juvenile swallows chattered from their nests in the roof of the porch and outside the sun beat down on an impressive grey marble monument.

As I walked away I heard the swifts screaming and the laughter of the children rising from the nearby playfield. Then I saw behind the moment the bright faces of Jasmine Lewthwaite and little Amy Beadel, and all the future of my kind throughout the world wherever humanity and Nature meet in celebration.

Village Characters No. 8
The Veteran footballer
Johnny Coombes of Combeinteignhead, Devon

Combeinteignhead

The name has fascinated me since childhood when I found the place by accident while exploring the tidal reaches of the River Teign.

Combeinteignhead is quite a mouthful for such a small community, but the village comes as a pleasant surprise to the visitor motoring from Newton Abbot to Shaldon.

You take the bend and the thatch is waiting at the roadside to seduce the tourist.

Westborough Cottage stood under the gleam of its new thatch – a Beauty Spot Calendar property it would be difficult to ignore. Maybe it was a bit of that Merry England created by the Victorians as an antidote to the grim reality of 19th Century rural life.

Combeinteignhead isn't a working village. There used to be three farms in the community. Now there's just the one, Cliff Chudleigh's Westborough near the cottage of the same name as you enter the village.

The old rural sights and smells crowded in as I wandered among the outhouses and byres. The morning traffic was building up on the busy road, but the past had its own life beneath the old red tiles and corrugated iron, in glooms full of farm machinery and bags of animal feed.

There was a handy carpark next to the Village Hall and the M'sieur Hulot tennis court with its Fifties air. Across the way an unpretentious cottage stood on the hillside next to a cider apple orchard.

I walked into the village, past traditional architecture and masses of traditional roses. It was all very comforting and the cars roaring by merely accentuated the 'backwater' atmosphere.

Up on the roof of Chantry Cottage, Richard Pascoe, the thatcher from Bickington, tapped down another sheaf of straw. He was never short of work as more and more newcomers decided to cap their rural dream with thatch.

Nearby Spring Cottage and Cayzers were superb examples of the thatcher's art. Above them the swifts swooped and cruised through sunshine silted with winged insects.

But Coombe Hatch Guest House had a seaside quality you don't expect to find in the country although the sea was only a few miles away. The row of small dwellings a little further on were reminders of a working past. They were now desirable properties.

Beyond them was a splendid vegetable garden lying under nets and sunlight and the drone of bees. Then another row of farm workers' cottages reminded me of my terrace house boyhood with the zinc bath and the lav in the yard and dad washing at the sink.

Above the lofty hedge to the right was the sandstone rectory and its gables and weather vane. On the bend below it were more modest buildings and a stream called the River Dod. This 'River', which an infant could jump, was perhaps one of those Celtic exaggerations of the physical world – part of the nomenclature of wishful thinking!

At the Post Office Stores Mrs Jacqui Reith was pottering about in her little parlour of a shop.

'It caters for everyone,' she grinned. 'You get to know what people want and you keep it on your shelves.'

Every village shop is different in its own way yet each carries the same goods – the tins of petfood, curry meals in packets, jars of sweets, newspapers, stamps, bottles of booze.

While Jacqui dodged into the back room for a crafty cup of tea I went to speak to Mr Stan White in his amazing garden that was once part of a farm. He was turning the hose on a flower show it would be hard to rival. Such displays should be the pride of the community.

Encircling the riot of African Marigolds and less exotic blooms was a five inch gauge model railway track.

'I run the steam engine for my grandchildren,' Stan said.

The engine, named Adam after a grandson, was being admired by another grandson called Matthew.

Out in the street Billy Smith, who works at Westborough Farm, was holding up the traffic and leading a flock of sheep past Coombe Garage. Farmer Chudleigh was bringing up the rear in a Land Rover.

I turned right where the sign pointed the way to The Wild Goose Inn. Combeinteignhead's climate of quiet affluence registered at either hand with the sort of properties you see advertised in *Country Life*. One of the locals told me it was 'commuter haven', a rural anchorage for doctors, dentists and assorted business folk.

Village life is organic and among the lovely houses there weren't many holiday homes. Combeinteignhead hadn't rented out its heritage. It had changed with the time, but was still a village people lived in and loved.

A wayside nook lured me through the lych gates into the graveyard of All Saints Church to walk among the headstones and wild angelica. The church had a sandstone tower, a clock, a fine well-kept interior and around 900 years of history which the wood pigeons were celebrating with a low crooning.

My walkabout brought me past white buildings with black paintwork to The Wild Goose Inn which was also white with black paintwork. The notice outside told me the landlord provided good food, good ale and good wine; but it was too early to sample the fare.

Printed on the misted glass of the bar window were the words Country House Inn. Maybe this hinted at an identity problem although the bugling of domestic geese from a nearby garden lent the current name a glow of authenticity. But the closeness of the Teign might be a more obvious link.

I strolled on between cottages, a few bungalows, big gardens and thatch galore. Lang Barn Farm was now Lang Barn Forge and blacksmith Derek Ambridge not only sent the sparks flying, but was also the guardian of the community cider press. His wife Carol performs with the Combeinteignhead

Heather and Gorse Clog Dancers. She was in her costume ready for the Sidmouth Folk Festival. Derek was in his forge.

'I do mostly wrought iron work,' he said, showing me the power hammer and the rest of the paraphernalia necessary to the production of things like fire hoods.

I recalled the autumn I had come here to take part in the cider making and to drink the excellent farmhouse rough while the little co-operative of seven families attended to the business of turning apples into scrumpy.

Derek told me Johnny Coombes lived up the road in Albert Cottage. I knew Johnny from the South Devon soccer circuit. He used to play for Stokeinteignhead and Windsor United and hadn't changed much since we last met on the field. He was a 48-year-old red soil local whose dad, Ernie, once drove the horsedrawn bread delivery van for Fowlers.

'The place has changed,' Johnny said. 'The baker's shop has gone and so have the market gardens which used to be in the centre of the village. There aren't many born and bred villagers left either, but it's the same all over and I've got good neighbours. It's a good little village.'

And Combeinteignhead was a visual feast with Home House a white architectural masterpiece set above a tree-choked valley where the River Dod flowed and willow leaves whitened in the breeze.

Beyond the converted out-buildings and lost-forever byres of what had once been Gulmswell Farm the land wound into the South Devon countryside. The swifts filled the morning with that most summery of sounds, but Combeinteignhead was a village for all seasons.

Lustleigh

It was approaching noon and the day was hot as I came past Kelly Farm and let the signpost direct me towards the village.

Big summer clouds drifted over from Dartmoor, but the swifts had gone leaving reaches of silence in the sky where they had hunted a week or so ago.

If I had consulted the standard guide books I would have been heading for the Old Manor House at Mapstone or Foxworthy, Foxworthy Mill and South Harton which are fine

Village Characters No 9
Wendy from the Dairy
Lustleigh . Devon

17th century farmhouses; or maybe I'd have settled for a browse around Waye and Higher Hisley which also guarantee granite delights, but I wanted to 'discover' Lustleigh for myself. I wanted to poke around in those unsung corners which tell you a lot about a village.

Beyond a reedy meadow, houses in gardens and a row of cottages full of moorland character I stood before the War Memorial. The names of the dead were inscribed in black lettering on granite. 'Lest we forget,' the epitaph proclaimed. Cars passed. Birds were singing. Another summer was slowly coming to an end.

A little further on the road dipped and divided leaving the church stranded among a crop of granite crosses on its own island of grass. Cider apples were ripening in the sun on my left and I walked in that direction towards the thatch.

Lustleigh is one of those villages you find in coffee table books entitled 'Beautiful Britain' or 'Britain's Rural Heritage'. People travel a long way to see it, for it possesses everything the rural romantic requires, en passant of course!

There's the thatch, the flower gardens, a tea garden, pub, beer garden, church, orchards; historic farms, corner shops and a cricket field. There is also a gentle vitality in the lifestyle.

Some for whom quietness is a penance might feel the atmosphere was more 'laid to rest' than 'laid back'. My grandfather told me never to move to a village without long self-examination.

Most people do not need a surfeit of peace and quiet. What is paradise to the genuine country person can be miserable boredom to others less committed to everything a rural life implies.

I sauntered by a house with the sort of attractive rickety porch stray cats love to doze in, and came to The Cleave Hotel, a 15th century inn. The sun beat down on the lawns and flower beds of the beer garden while I resisted the temptation to sink a pint and walked on.

At the bend was a big granite cross standing in a bit of rough grass. I sat down and took some photographs of a couple of cottages with a couple of tourists admiring the thatch, but ignoring the nearby Gospel Hall.

This was a small brick building wearing brown paint and a serious Sunday air. 'Lords Day Observance architecture,' my dad would have called it. Behind me the shop that dealt in antiques and teas had a thatched roof and a much more worldly exterior.

I went down some steps and around by the Gospel Hall into a corner full of roses and thatch. Then another corner brought me to the old railway bridge and the River Wray.

It was a 'river' many a stream would laugh at. I grinned happily at the thought of the Celt who had pumped up his corner of the living world to heroic dimensions.

Anyway, it was a lovely nut-brown brook running beside the path and the cricket field. Geographically I had left Lustleigh and was in the hamlet of Wreyland. But I could have wandered through one of Rupert Brooke's sonnets into an Edwardian idyll.

On the right-hand side were impressive properties and three kids messing about in an inflatable on the river. Children's voices, birdsong and the sound of running water threaded through the leafy hush.

Beyond the walnut tree I came upon a group of beautiful cottages. One of them, Lower Wreyland, had a charming thatched porch but it could not compete with the house opposite whose granite porch made my skin prickle. In this white dwelling, Wreyland Manor, everything had been orchestrated to produce everyone's idea of the country cottage.

Wisteria climbed the walls, the paintwork was black, the thatch old yet healthy and beside the deep porch and its tiny cobbles was a pump and a horsetrough. Lustleigh Church clock chimed the hour of noon and out of this astonishing house came Mr Wellstead and his two rough-haired Jack Russells – Salt and Pickles. The dogs proved to be very amiable little animals, not at all like my own peppery terrier.

Even the outbuildings of Wreyland were thatched and it was great to discover a car parked in a thatched garage. Walking back towards Lustleigh I suspected Wreyland was really a part of Lewis Carol's Wonderland which the author chose to leave unadvertised.

The cattle on the hillside beyond Wrey Villa, the flower scent and greenness were far removed from the urban beat with its graffiti, betting shops, takeaways and unremarkable housing. Here the living world was part of things. It didn't just intrude in the shape of a feral pigeon or a town fox or a butterfly dancing above a window box.

If you opt for village life you opt for neighbourliness within a close-knit society. My own experience of it in the past presented me with those little acts of kindness which restore your faith in humanity, and gossip which can hurt and that sensation of someone always looking over your shoulder into your existence. In every sense you belong to the community and I suppose you only get out what you put in.

Across the road from the Post Office Store I bought some ripe Stilton in the Dairy. Wendy and James Manners-Chapman, the proprietors, were a pleasant young couple.

Wendy was a Lustleigh girl with an open face and the sort of smile that's good for trade. Her Stilton was strong enough to stand up and sing; her shop one of the finest examples of a village store I've ever set foot in.

Walking up to the church I could imagine the changing seasons registering as dramatic events in Lustleigh with all the traditional English country things thriving – the whistdrives, garden fetes and flower shows.

Being a rural romantic I was comforted by these notions although as a visitor I was only scratching the surface of village life. Lustleigh seemed to stand aloof from outside events, but maybe this was another illusion.

Dogs barked at each other from the back seats of parked

cars. People came, admired the thatched cottages, aimed their cameras at the thatched cottages, smiled appreciatively, ate tea, perhaps, or drank beer, then departed.

I would have liked to have spent a long time in the Church of St John the Baptist, but I was dying for a pint. I liked the roses on the lych gate roof and the dark little interior of the building which seems impossibly old, but the beer garden of The Cleave Hotel pandered to the pagan in me.

The pub has a friendly barmaid in Alison. She was serving customers while other members of the staff ferried in the lunchtime platters. Several cravats and their spouses had gathered to sample the cuisine in the cheerful little bar.

Here I found all the essentials of a real pub. It was a good place to take my leave of Lustleigh and prepare the spirit for the change of social climate you find in Torbay.

Cockington

Cockington is one of those hybrid communities where the ingredients of nostalgia simmer in a kind of market place atmosphere.

There's cricket on the green in front of historic Cockington

Village Characters No. 10
Bill Wakeham, Retired Cowman
Cockington, Devon.

Court and horse-drawn traps carry you into another age at 75p per trip.

There are farms and fowls, ducks, horses and work dogs, middens, thatch, cows and a nice bit of the Devonshire burr. All these are elements of rural continuity which the tides of the holiday trade leave untouched.

And this is a curious phenomenon. What remains of yesterday is life-giving. The rest has that seasonal feel peculiar to all tourist areas.

One thing is certain: Cockington is still a hamlet. It isn't part of Torquay and even the strong commercial side is preferable to the catch-penny parades of its big neighbour or Paignton's Torbay Road.

I left the car in the car park and ambled off through the sunshine. The clop of horses' hooves beat across the cooing of pigeons. Beyond the thatch was Cockington Wood.

Few people were about, but the No Parking signs everywhere hinted at traffic problems and crowds. The Mill Cafe over the road had a gravel courtyard and wooden garden furniture and a few small reminders of the previous day's business in its litter.

The refreshment area was large and Mid-Atlantic, the sort of thing you might expect to find in a Disneyland village. Yet from the trees behind the cafe a green woodpecker cried.

Around the corner by the shops leading to the ponds were the lawns and flower beds of The Drum Inn. To my left the water wheel stood unmoving in a dark niche.

Up by the ponds which were marky and fishless Mr and Mrs Redman from Humberside were watching the ducks.

'It's a nice place,' said Mrs Redman. 'It's what city people think a country village should be.'

'There's a lot of character left,' said her husband.

A micro-light glider passed overhead as unobtrusively as a motorbike snarling up the aisle of Westminster Abbey!

The Snow brothers, Chris and Ian, who were tidying the Drum Inn gardens with their dad, Dennis, broke off for a minute to chat to me. The gardening was their Sunday job, and the lawns and flowerbeds were a testament to Dennis's skill and the lads' graft. Mr Snow had seen five different landlords at The Drum.

The inn was pure 1930's brick and thatch – a stockbroker-belt pub planted in a Devon setting. But it had a presence and was unashamedly suburban-rural.

In the bar, I met the landlord, Mr Vince Horseley, and his wife Janet. Vince is a Devonian whose trade is mainly seasonal. At peak periods he employs up to 35 staff.

'The place was designed by Sir Edwin Lutyens,' he told me. 'It was built in 1936.'

On the walls were big, framed photographs of foxhunt meets outside the pub – circa pre-hunt saboteur days. The clatter of horses' hooves brought the scenes to life, but it came from the road and I went out to meet two drivers seated on their horse-drawn hackney cabs.

They were Debbie Moore of Newton Abbot and her friend Claire Hale of Cockington – a couple of very attractive young ladies. I asked them to tell me about their job.

'I drive a horse and cart,' Debbie laughed. 'It's as simple as that.' And with great success, I bet, I thought as the pair set their traps rolling expertly down the hill.

The stamp and grind of hooves is part of Cockington's charm. It pursued me when I came up to have a look at the Almshouses.

In the weed-choked bullock yard behind them Bill Wakeham was peering under the bonnet of a car with his son Brian. Bill has just retired after a working life as Cowman, mainly with the Denbow brothers at what was Home Farm. He recalled the yard when it was full of animal life.

'Us had bullocks in the great house over yonder,' he said. 'And pigs in the piggeries.'

He would collect the swill from Paignton, bring it back to the yard, boil it and feed it to the pigs.

'I had a cattle dug (dog),' he said. 'Poor old Bounce is daid now but backalong me and he would get in the cows, all year round, all weathers – even when twas pitch black.'

Swallows gathered on the guttering above the eaves of the stock buildings.

'I'd drive 40 to 50 cows along the road,' Bill continued. 'And in the summer it would take ages to get past the forge. The crowds was so big, you see.'

An hour had passed since I had left the car but the tourists were already queuing outside the Mill Café and the carpark was nearly full. The cricket match had begun at Cockington Court and when the churchbells rang out the jigsaw of the past came together.

Cockington Lane was the way back through the decades to my childhood, the cottages by the smithy were full of the Devon accent and the gardens were full of flowers. The Court itself had been the home of the Mallock family, and before that a possession of the Careys of Torre Abbey.

Standing near the Court the old church with its 14th century screen and 15th century font had a thousand years of history in its foundations. The bells and the horse-drawn traps reversed the flow of time.

Down by the Forge Reg Pitts of Lanscombe Farm sat in his trap between runs to the sea-front and back. Beside him was another cabman, Derek Shore, and Derek's horse, Tina. Holidaymakers were milling about searching for opportunities to spend money.

They were unaware that this was Prudential Village. Like most of the other businesses the Forge was leased from the Prudential Insurance Society. An odd state of affairs but entirely in keeping with the oddness of the place!

When I was a kid a blacksmith worked at the Forge. Now the open front glowed with brass gifts and souvenirs. I visited the Weavers Cottage and I walked around Court Cottage Pottery and Rose Cottage gift shop before wandering on to Lanscombe Farm where about ten years ago I bought my rough-haired Jack Russell, James.

The Pitts' daughter, Heather, runs a riding stables from the yard but Reg still keeps cows and calves at Meadow Farm up past The Drum. His wife, Ruby, is a country lady in the South Devon tradition – polite, good-natured, unassuming.

Rural smells eddied around the buildings. In the road in front of the farm families were admiring the ducks and the stream. Cars crept by. The traps rolled back and forth behind placid horses. Reg lifted a hand in greeting.

It was astonishing – the country flavour of places like Lanscombe and the bullock yard by the Almshouses. Bill Wakeham, the Horseleys, the Pitts and their neighbours Iris Foreman and Yvonne Rawlings helped keep it alive.

They could still distance themselves from the commercialism. Iris and Yvonne had a smallholding where the animals were pets and the horses' names were printed on the stable doors.

In the hamlet, like the rest of Torbay, tourism was the name of the game, but Cockington is a community in its own right. It must never be engulfed by urban expansion.

CHAPTER FOUR

Food and Drink

Apples

The homemade pie – September is one of the magic months. It looks back on summer's fullness and forward to autumn's slow striptease.

At the end of the month you are aware of Earth Mother taking off her clothes with a flourish before presenting her nakedness to winter winds. After luxury and wantonness comes the sackcloth and ashes. Even as a child I wondered why we imposed aspects of human frailty on Nature.

It was as if the human condition was the common denominator of creation – and here I am falling into the vanity of it all again – Mother Nature, Father Time, human life as a parable or metaphor when in reality mankind exists within eternal continuities which are magnificently indifferent to human affairs.

Yet this remains true; September is the month of spider-spin. The strands between the wall and hedge in our back lane cling to the faces of the postman and milkman as they do their early morning rounds. September is also the month of flocking birds with starlings passing in dark clouds over the countryside.

In my garden the big striped spiders cover the hedges with gossamer deathtraps for the bees. Mornings and evenings are cool and about this time of year I start wearing a sweater although it usually isn't cold enough for a jacket.

Beyond Torbay the harvest has been brought home and there's only scorched stubble to remind us of a season gone up in smoke. The countryside is silent under heavy dews. Soon the Harvest Festival hymns will complete the requiem for summer and perhaps the corn dollies will bring urban communities close to their roots. The blackberries, bullens and dog hips are part of the splendour.

Whenever I cast my mind back to childhood Septembers I

see the hedges of Clennon full of berries and birds. Yesterday tends to creep into my thoughts to eclipse the present but in writing this I'm not trying to exorcize ghosts; I'm actually exercising ghosts – bringing the shadows out of the shadows.

Once upon a time, in Devon B.D. (Before the Developers), my mother and I went mushrooming and blackberrying in Clennon Valley. Then there were elms rocking in the gales of the summer equinox and herons in the drainage guts and cattle in the watermeadows.

At dimpsey I ran home to find the kitchen as bright as Aladdin's Cave and the apple pie out of reach of the cats. After the stew the pie was served with clotted cream and my parents chatted across the chink of cutlery, the odd belch and the crackle of the fire.

So, September is also about apple pie and the warmth of family life – doodles in the margins of eternity; but maybe in the final analysis God looks beyond the general to the particular and the apple pie and the family dwarf the cosmic drama.

Jacket Potatoes

The gales of the autumn equinox were filling the air above Clennon Valley with birds and leaves. Flocks of starlings scattered over the reedbeds and the pines beside the stream that divided the water meadows were thrashing and roaring. The gleam of rain lay on the plough. Gulls speckled the dark soil and the corn ricks at the top of Stuggy Lane were full of sparrows.

1947 was the golden year of my childhood. I was ten and Clennon Valley was always waiting down the road to feed my happiness or brush away my sorrows. Herons stalked the drainage ditches, foxes kennelled in the reeds, thousands of wild duck visited the floodwater. Snipe and woodcock shared wild corners with the moorhens, and barn owls nested in the ruined linhay at the bottom of the field under Tanner's Lane.

As kids we came here to scrump apples and plums, lift potatoes and swedes from the clamps, to bird nest and poach, and swing from the creepers in New Road Forest. The stream was fresh and clear then although it ran eventually through the town dump.

The owls quartered the smoking acres of rubbish and foxes also took rats and rabbits from the garbage. Here the urban world ended in stench and confusion. Beyond it were water-meadows, copses, tall hedges and grazing that climbed the high hill to Crabb's Park.

That September had already brought a little gold to the bracken and yellowed a few leaves. After a couple of weeks of rain the air was cool and the sun shone without warmth through the easterly wind. Out on the bay the waves broke white and surf climbed up the beaches.

Five buzzards cut their circles in the sky over the wood and beat down the valley into the gale. The sun had gone and evening was crumbling to dimpsey. I sat under the oak tree on the hill as the stars came out and the meadows vanished beneath mist. Eventually the hunger gurgling in my stomach drove me home and I came in to find Mam taking the jacket potatoes from the oven. Each King Edward surrendered a puff of fragrance as it was opened. Then the butter melted into those little pits and pockets of flavour that made me shake my head and smile like a wolf.

Fish and Chips

We rarely had fish and chips as a main meal in our house when I was a boy but sometimes Friday was the exception. Mam took working class pride in getting up a cooked tea for her husband, but looking back I wonder how much she was shackled to the stove and mangle as dad was shackled to the workbench.

Certainly she spent the greater part of each day scrubbing the front steps, washing, ironing, shopping, cleaning and cooking. She also catered for summer visitors so we could have the extras middle class families took for granted; but we never had a family holiday. Living at the seaside seemed to make that event unnecessary.

We spent a lot of time in the fields beyond Torbay, for Mam was a country girl, the daughter of a Welsh salmon fisherman. She knew where the best mushrooms grew and could always find the juiciest blackberries. On blowy September days we roamed the top of Clennon Valley and on towards Waddeton filling our baskets while she chattered endlessly, firing my imagination, making me want to set it down on paper as drawings or prose.

It is a mistake to think that an only child is a lonely child. My parents were my companions. They gave me a lot of attention. Both were intelligent and could cope with my curiosity until I got to grammar school and started asking really difficult questions.

Fridays and Saturdays were the best days of the week. If I was home from school sick or on holiday or just mitching I was left free to get muddy out in the countryside. Sometimes I would cycle down to the Dart at Aish duck marsh and walk the banks of the river till dimpsey. I stayed well after dark to prolong the happiness. I knew dad would be smarting himself up for beer and darts at the Torbay Inn and Mam would be putting the guard in front of the fire.

Later I would stand in the queue outside St Michaels Road chip shop and get my three-pennyworth and scribbles shot into a dunce's cap of newspaper. Then I would eat them in the pub doorway and wait for dad to bring me out a glass of sweet cider. I never wanted Friday night to end.

Apples: The Wild Crab

Leaving the meadow on the headland I walked between bracken and gorse towards the cave and the wooded coombe. On the steeps between the path and the clifftops were sycamores and blackthorn. Then the sea ran through sun-dazzle all the way to the horizon and the sort of sky that comes alive at night with hosts of stars.

Beyond the last hawthorn was the crab tree loaded with its little wild apples which were pale yellow, flushed with scarlet.

The wild crab stood about 12 feet high. Dwarf trees like this were the ancestors of superb cultivated apples such as Laxton's Fortune, Bramleys and Cox's Orange Pippins.

I picked up one of the windfalls and bit into it. The bitterness exceeded that of the harshest cider apple I've ever tasted. I can recall many an occasion in the past when I was grateful to this tree on a warm autumn day. Later it would play host to a variety of birds and the badgers that lived in the setts on the steeps would greedy the windfalls.

The crab was one of those links with prehistory which always delight and excite my imagination. Bronze Age man would have eaten its fruit and maybe even drank the fermented juice although 'verjuice' as it's called, isn't to be recommended as a beverage! Somehow time loses its significance when you think of a prehistoric hunter standing before similar trees and gathering some of the hard, sour apples.

I like summer-leafing British trees, especially the stunted sort which thrive in seawinds on the South Devon coast — blackthorn, sycamore, willow, sallow, hawthorns, and, of course, the odd crab. Unlike the apple tree in your garden, the wild variety has thorns and the name crab is a corruption of the Norse 'skrab' meaning scrubby.

Anyway, I sat under the crab tree and watched seabirds flapping over the mussel reefs just offshore. The wind had risen and every so often a small apple fell at my feet. Autumn was beginning to edit the landscape.

Apples: Agricultural Wine

Now that the cider apples are ripening towards the gathering and the pressing I think of my father and the threshold of other autumns.

I suppose his vision of heaven or Valhalla or whatever Nirvana he subscribed to centred on the big sherry casks in Charlie Crang's barn where the apple juice matured to brain-numbing potency. The fumes rising from a tapped barrel would anaesthetize passing birds and bring a dozy smile to the faces of old ladies in gardens a good mile away.

Can they really have gone forever, those days of agricultural wine and noses? It is impossible to forget the purple, potato conks pitted with tiny acid holes and covered in a mesh of broken blood vessels.

Scrumpy, or farmhouse rough as my old man preferred to call it, has acquired a bad reputation because it has been quaffed by unwary holiday-makers or 'lads' out on a spree.

My dad drank it with respect in the company of the other

connoisseurs who inhabited the rural margins of Paignton in those days. If it conferred leglessness on occasions such a condition was achieved cheerfully.

But the old man never needed excuses to head for Crang's sherry casks. September of wasps and windfalls, scrumpy-loosened kneecaps, teeth and bowels, provided the agricultural wine central to a Celtic clan happening.

In the early autumn the orchards of Waterside were magnificent with apples hanging like thousands of Chinese lanterns – red, scarlet and crimson. For dad they were symbols of liquid plenitude and Crang's barn was a shrine in the middle of a living festival of fruit.

Fortunately the old man wasn't respectable. He was too in love with life to bother about the gossip or the dreary conformity which can suffocate small communities.

According to his simple philosophy Earth Mother was a rosy-cheeked matron with a wicked sense of humour and an apron full of goodies. Naturally she liked her tipple. You only had to look at the sozzled pigs in the orchards scoffing the windfalls to realise the pleasure she derived from playing tricks on the most unlikely creatures.

Dad was a child of his age, harmless, good-natured, loving, and he was over eighty when he died. Right up to the last week of his life he was sinking pints of the primrose-coloured tangle-foot which, he claimed, had kept him 'loose, lucid and lively for the best part of a century'.

Tonight I'm going to open a flagon of the best farmhouse rough and salute his memory.

Pubs and Cider

My dad was Scrumpty-Dumpty. In the summer when he sweated he leaked rough cider and the wasps homed in on him like Exocets.

For him there was no music sweeter than the squeak of the tap turning in the barrel followed by the gush of the potent juice filling his sleever.

Rough cider, cool from the wood, can seal a day of hot sunshine, larksong, the shrill of swallows, dusty lanes and parched countryside.

My old man paddled down the wild rivers of scrumpy to hit the apple high at watering holes around Torbay. He could wax lyrical about mature cheddar, raw onion and a quart of Churchwards liquid gold on the garden bench at the end of a long working day; and I swear he would have crawled a thousand miles over broken glass to suck the pap out of a rotting Kingston Black.

Cider is a West Country drink. It goes with apple orchards, villages, thatch, the smell of cattle in summer lanes and the sort of thirsts that spring from hard outdoor work.

When I was young and went in for casual farmwork like picking peas or corn harvesting, the cider jar was a feature of the day's toil in the sun. Now the taste of Churchward's rough reminds me of those summer days and old characters long gathered to their forefathers. I see the knuckles whitening to tilt the jar and hear the work horses snorting to blow the dust off the oats in their nose bags and the heat of a long-gone July breaks over me.

Often in the early days when I was struggling to make a living as a writer I cycled or walked to the Church House Inn at Stoke Gabriel and sat outside chatting to Marshall Baker while I swigged the cider he had tapped.

That village pub is still a sanctuary for the Devon accent. The phantoms of the Forties still gather here for euchre and when I go out to the lav I sometimes bump into my dad's ghost as he lurches back to the snug for the jokes and the laughter and 'agricultural wine' with the 'buyh'.

Little has changed, thank God. The salmon still splash about in the fishermen's yarns and the accent's get broader whenever a holidaymaker lingers, baffled, at the euchre table. The Stoke Gabriel Mafia are in control. It's still Cosa Nostra, ma boodie. Still, ''ow be 'ackin', buyh,' as someone 'sits' or 'tries it'.

CHAPTER FIVE

Devon Landscapes

Hills and Coombe

I love Long Combe. Early in the morning before the traffic builds up on Totnes Road I sometimes stand west of Ayreville and look down into that green and pleasant coombe. Away to the left is Lomentor Copse on its hillside.

My vantage point is over 300 feet high and I am well above the rooftops of Higher Longcombe, Middle Longcombe and Longcombe – all of which are little muddles of dwellings. Perhaps the scene is quintessential South Devon – the small green fields, the red soil, the brook dividing the valley before it finds the Dart at Fleet Mill Reach.

For visitors to the county the coombe lying between rounded hills with their crowns of trees must be a microcosm of the Devonshire countryside. Rooks come cawing across

gulfs of sunlight and often a buzzard circles and mewls against the blue summer sky.

This place is one of those corners of my boyhood that remains unmolested. Away on the right beyond the road is Rypen Copse and Rypen Clump. Glazegate Lane climbs towards the Berry Pomeroy road and at the bottom of the combe the Stoke Gabriel Road winds uphill past Parliament Cottage where William of Orange stopped en route to London in 1688.

But I look across the repository of my own past. When I was little I came here and pretended I was Henry William's 'Crow Starver' in the story of the same name although I loved rooks, those 'old blacktops' which even today you can come across hanging lifeless on a barbed wire fence.

Long Combe is part of my consciousness as a Westcountry-man. I can sit listening to music in my garden and let it form to clarity behind my eyes. And I confess that often while I am driving back from the Hebrides in the spring or autumn a vision of the coombe has strengthened my love of home.

October Journey

Yesterday I heard the cows lowing in the milking shed of Grange Court Farm although the farm and the animals are no more.

Along the edge of memory cocks crowed and the shires snuffled and stamped and ducks paddled across the liquid manure in the bullock yard. The stubble fires had left the hill black but the plough was laying bare soil the colour of ox blood. The cowman whistled, children ran laughing down Stuggy Lane and the lovely October day settled on its beauty.

Often I wonder why the valley continues to haunt me. It was not a remarkable place as Dartmoor or the sea cliffs are remarkable, but it played host to my childhood although that in itself is not reason enough for the joy and sadness recollection can kindle.

The stream, the watermeadows, the copses, hedges, hills and lanes provided everything I needed in those days. Time had a glacial drift and autumn seemed to last forever. My senses could hardly cope with the thrill of the open air at dawn and dimpsey. Beginnings and endings always left me light-headed waiting for the miraculous to sweep me into something I could never label.

Well, yesterday I was scuffing through drifts of fallen leaves again in the lane that climbed through orchards to the field which was white with mushrooms. Some of the morning's mist still clung to the spiderspin and bees hummed and danced about the ivy blossom.

Low and golden through golden leaves shone the sun. Across the valley went flocks of starlings, pigeons and gulls. Golds and browns darkened and dimpsey was rich with the smell of woodsmoke, cattle dung and damp soil.

Then there were the barn owls peddling their loneliness to lonely people and the foxes screaming and rooks clotting the treetops. Perhaps somewhere at sometime our human and animal selves cease to be separate entities and unite to share a spirit life fed by the beauty of the world.

At Clennon when I was a boy the seasons were great adventures. It is possible to love a landscape so deeply you feel you are that place. Then the past colours the present and yesterday lives again.

Alone and Together

I was dropped off at Okehampton camp to walk the military road on to the blanket bog. Snow had fallen and the wilderness was white. The surface water between peat hags was frozen and walking wasn't difficult. A light wind sent the snow powder hissing faintly away.

Soon I was beyond the wellhead of the river with the day brightening. The Upper East Dart was a sky-coloured ribbon of water running through solitudes which were hazed in silence.

It snaked through the empty hills, taking me with it to somewhere else. Bleak, lonely coutryside always has this effect on me. It registered as a warm ache around the heart.

Dartmoor had become once again the landscape of promise that gave me the chance to relate to self and the wilderness rather than to people. There are few of these places left in England where you can wander for miles without encountering a fellow human being. Paradoxically the experience usually brings me closer to humanity.

At Postbridge, with the moor's most famous clapper bridge, people take over again even in winter. Then it is good to sit awhile and drink something hot from the flask, watching the children spellbound by the combination of snow and running water. For most of the boys and girls the winter trip to Dartmoor will be remembered for years afterwards as The Great Adventure.

Even without summer holiday weather there is a definite human warmth about the little crowd. It springs from the freedom of it all and the seemingly foreverness of the place.

That toddle along the riverbank, near the road and never far from the parked car will endure as a trek into real wilderness. In its own way the moor feeds most human needs.

Hills of Childhood: The Sugar Loaf (Goodrington, near Paignton)

The hills of childhood seemed much bigger when I was at primary school but in those days all adults loomed large as giants and a double-decker bus was something colossal.

In 1944 we moved to a house in Grosvenor Terrace and I became the youngest member of the Fisher Street gang.

Paignton, like the rest of Torbay, was full of American servicemen. Jeeps, 'ducks' and lorries were the most familiar transport on the roads and at the top of the beaches there were the metal structures of defences thrown up to thwart enemy landings. Beyond these were the coiled barbed wire.

But 1944 was a year of optimism. Rumours of the impending invasion of Europe lent a new edge to our defiance and my own parochial world began to expand.

That spring we came along Goodrington Sands past the ships which had been beached for keel scrubbing and followed the path beside the railway line.

A steam engine puffed by, pulling goods trucks. Gulls flapped out of the smoke.

Out in the bay smoke was also billowing from the funnels of warships. A motor torpedo boat furrowed the water as it raced towards Brixham.

We came to the little headland above Saltern Cove and climbed the monkey pole. Then we returned to the path and walked the final fifty yards to the Sugar Loaf.

The wind was coming lightly off the bay and the sky was cloudless.

Eric led us up the gentle slope through the new bracken and primroses to the top of that small, rounded hill.

Below was the lovely little goyal which would soon be covered in caravans. It was apple green. Rabbits ran off with a flash of scuts. Overhead a buzzard circled and loosed its cries.

I was on my first real hill, one of those wild little heights in the sky.

There among the old bracken stabs, I found the skull of a stoat. It was sunbleached white and all the tiny teeth were intact.

Carefully I wrapped it in my hanky to carry it home.

I still have it, among the other animal skulls and the feathers in my study.

Sometimes when I handle it or draw it that first visit to the Sugar Loaf comes alive again.

Hills of Childhood: Clennon Hill (above Clennon Valley, Paignton).

The winter of 1947 transformed my valley. The familiar water meadows and hills became an arctic waste. The canal and stream froze and the skinny bodies of birds lay where the creatures had starved to death.

The snowy pastures were dotted with fieldfares, redwings, bramblings and lapwings. The awful north wind ruffled the feathers. Sometimes I picked up one that was still alive but too weak to fly.

Then I would gently ease it under my vest in the hope my body heat would restore its strength. But it always died and I came heartbroken through the snow-phantoms which the wind was sending across the whiteness. These phantoms were like the dust-devils of the American prairies; only they were composed of snow powder.

Clennon was deserted. Duck flighted down to the frozen levels. Several skidded across the ice and ended up in embarrassed heaps, leaving me laughing helplessly.

Clennon Ponds

At the top of the valley to the left of the New Road Forest was the high ground I called Clennon Hill. The summit runs now into Roselands Estate but in the Forties there were fields all the way to Higher Yalberton and there were no housing estates and industrial estates.

I recall the heartbreak when the STC factory covered the lovely meadows where the brown hares had run. Of course change is inevitable and all communities expand. There is no having without loss and no love without grief.

That late afternoon, with the snow glare all around me and the sky black above, I climbed through the drifts, over the crunchy whiteness to the great tree near the top. Then I leaned against the bole and felt the tree shuddering in the wind.

The whole of Clennon Valley stretched below me like a corner of Siberia. The town dump had vanished. Whiteness stood mounded at either hand in the bottom of the sky.

There was the ice-glazed marsh and the stream and dykes; there were the linhays and orchards and hedges I loved. There were no caravans, no Penwill Way, no housing estates.

When the thaw came the badgers would roam their trails where Roselands now sprawls. The farm animals would graze where the houses of Penwill Way now stand.

But at least the hill remains bracken clad and free from development as part of the Clennon Nature Reserve.

I suppose it is my 'Fern Hill' and when I climb it now I see the funeral of my childhood and ache for the way things were.

Near Cranmere Pool

The military road up from Okehampton Camp has opened up the northern wilderness and throughout the year there are always letterboxers at Cranmere Pool bending over the granite postbox. The 'pool' itself changes with the seasons. In the winter it can be a grim wind-blasted hollow full of black water and the ache of loneliness but the other day, under the rare sunlight of a wet disappointing summer, I was at Cranmere again with the grass silvering in the breeze; and I recalled other summer mornings when I had walked up the East Dart from Postbridge on to the high North Moor. The magnetism of the pool is undeniable. William Crossing discusses it in his *Gems in a Granite Setting* but for me it was a heartplace long before I discovered Crossing.

As a Devonian in love with wilderness Dartmoor, Cranmere was central to my consciousness. In fact, Henry Williamson brought the place into my knowing through *Tarka the Otter* and it became necessary for me as a boy to tread the animal's trail to the great Northern blanket bog where five rivers are born – the Tavy, Teign, Taw, Okement and East Dart. The solitude, desolation and secret wildlife were everything. The sheer physical presence of the tors and mire, the weather and the absence of human beings meant more to me than the history or prehistory of Dartmoor or any of the man-made paraphernalia littering the landscape. It registered as a sensation – the old nameless desire for the nameless place that has haunted me since childhood.

Last week the desire was tugging at my guts again. I wandered over the peat hags, jumping the patches of surface water and wading through the grass. Those delightful molluscs, the black slugs, clung to grass stems and there were frogs in the sphagnum moss and lizards wherever the going was drier. Winged insects clustered round my head and arms to greedy on the sweat. Then I put up two red grouse. Over the classic tundra flora of mosses, lichens and liverworts, the insects droned and buzzed and there was a constant patter of them on my skin.

Coming slowly up from the well-head of the East Dart I disturbed snipe and noted that absence of larksong peculiar to August. The cotton grass quivered in the wind, shaking out white silky tufts. It's Greek name is *Eriophorum* from Erion (cotton) and phora (bearing). The plant advertises mires but nowhere is the blanket bog dangerous although your chances of crossing it without wet feet are remote.

Finally, after a brief visit to Cranmere, I sat in the sun and listened to the scroak and cronk of ravens. All round me were the tors and acres of solitude. The absence of other human beings lent eloquence to the landscape but as always behind Nature I could hear Wordsworth's 'still, sad voice of humanity' and I was at peace with myself.

Cranmere

The East Dart flowed between Broad Down and Hartland Tor. White and bronze coloured water thundered through the strewn boulders, flexing its winter muscles.

Where it looped after leaving Stannon Tor behind it the beauty was uniquely West Country. Storm debris clouded the pools.

By the ancient hut one of the rowan trees held a crow's nest in spindly top branches. Above the waterfall near Sandy Hole Pass trees are rare.

At the Pass I met the mist but the sheep track ran parallel to the river and the walking was easy. The raw wind lent an edge to the trek. It put me in mind of days on Hebridean hills. Fine beads of moisture pearled my hair and clothes.

After Sandy Hole the walking was tougher. On both sides of the river were bogs and marshes. Crows attended me and as usual I put up snipe. Every so often I encountered sheep wearing expressions of desperation.

Most of the tributary streamlets were on the Broad Down bank and here I found great expanses of marsh and flooded ground. In an effort to avoid these booby traps I kept re-crossing the river. During the fording of one quiet place I startled a heron that lifted and became part of the mist.

The air grew cooler as I climbed towards the watershed. The mist was depressing and visibility was down to twenty yards. I rested in the ruins of a tin miner's hut and scoffed a Mars Bar.

The final stretch is always uplifting. I squelched through sphagnum bog, marsh and a web of streams. By the time I reached Cranmere I was soaked.

Cranmere in a cold mist was like the set of a gothic horror movie. There was no animal life although the mere is a stronghold of foxes.

Nothing stirred – except the slow thump of my heart. Then the wind was moaning in the cotton grass and the mist seemed to come to life and dance around me. I thought of my fox tribe – Wulfgar, Teg, Stargrief – all the fine animals that had ran out of my love of this Dartmoor wilderness to defeat time and age and death.

CHAPTER SIX

Moorland Views

The Great Ammil

Much of Dartmoor is between 1,000 and 2,000 feet above the sea. The rounded hills offer little resistance to the winter winds that whistle down from Siberia.

Despite its gentle appearance the terrain is capable of blizzards so violent they have become part of folk history. For those who lived through it the winter of 1947 is fresh in the mind.

It was a sort of biblical disaster, resulting in the 'Great Ammil'. Snow fell ceaselessly for days on end, piling up rooftop high and blocking the roads and railways.

Reservoirs and streams froze and the animals caught in the open were buried where they stood. Communities were cut off and villages and farms were without bread and milk. The moors became a vast graveyard, packed with the carcasses of sheep, ponies and cattle.

Becky Falls was solid and the waterfall at Lydford Gorge was another great downfall of ice. In the bottom of a leaden sky the tors were icebergs. Even the rabbits were dying of starvation and foxes were seen rooting under the snow on farmland after the cabbages.

The ice sheeting Leighon Ponds was littered with the bodies of redwings and fieldfares. Thousands of songbirds perished. Blizzards passed and were succeeded by other blizzards, and trees and telegraph poles crashed down. Then it began to drizzle.

The temperature was well below zero and the fine rain froze on contact with everything it touched. Presently the wind came strong from the north-east, turning the drizzle into an ice storm.

At first the verglas formed on the windward side of twigs, grasses, wire, reeds, rocks and branches, but when the storm died the drizzle fell steadily in a dense fog, covering the entire moor.

Twigs swelled to five times their normal circumference and blackthorn trees became heavy 'cut glass' sculptures. Branches were torn off by the weight of the ice; birches, rowans and beeches were brought down and telephone wires snapped. Reeds of ice stood beside stiff streams and the snowfields ran sparkling to ice-glazed tors.

All night and for most of the next day the moors were coated with ice which Devonians called the 'ammil'. The lethal beauty has never been surpassed.

Dartmoor looked as if it had been enamelled and perhaps 'ammil' is a corruption of 'enamel'.

Manaton Rocks

I am constantly surprised by the amazing variety of Dartmoor's tors, their different shapes and sizes, and domes and humps, stacks and steeples of granite.

Their rounded outlines can lend them the majesty of

Manaton Rocks   Brian Carter

sculptures often on a monumental scale in a setting that dwarfs anything the Tate Gallery can offer. They seem to have been placed deliberately on hilltops to catch the eye and lure the spirit.

That morning of early June I'd had enough of bleakness and desolation and after spending the dawn hours on the North Moor found myself at Manaton about the time civilised people take coffee.

I parked the car and walked up the footpath at the back of the church to Manaton Rocks. Crossing called this beautiful group of outcrops Manaton Tor and I wish the Ordnance Survey people would consult the master's work before committing themselves to print.

Anyway, these most shapely rocks are situated to the north of the village among scrub oak, rowan and holly. Their summits provide classic views of the in-country landscape with glimpses of nearby wilderness. Perhaps this is why I found them so appealing. They seemed to have been deliberately placed in a soft green corner of Dartmoor by an artist who knew what he was doing.

The rocks crown a low hill covered in walled fields. There are three main outcrops set well apart. One large rock occupies a corner of the grounds of Ebdon on private property.

I couldn't have chosen a better time of the year for my visit. The bluebells were radiant under the trees and the oak leaves more gold than green. The romance of the place was difficult to ignore. Birdsong, cattle belving and the splendid arrangement of the granite by courtesy of Time and Nature created a memorable experience.

Sitting up there I felt a little sad. Generations of village children had played among the rocks and these in-country tors, like country churches, have a way of bringing the past alive out of their silence.

Later I came down and walked around Manaton. It was one of the far outposts of my boyhood world and it's still a charming place. The Green is surrounded by trees and the granite church of St Winifred's has a 15th century traceried screen of carved oak.

Village cricket here is so English, elderly American tourists would have to recharge their pacemakers before soaking up the atmosphere. It's a heady cocktail of Thomas Hardy,

Edward Thomas and T. H. White. The local pub has a good all-year-round vitality and Manaton is solidly Dartmoor, cringing from the twee; but it wasn't the Church or Ford Farm with its celebrated ash house that came to mind as I motored home. I heard the wind once more in young oak leaves and caught the scent of the bluebells I'd left behind at Manaton Rocks.

The Rugglestone, Dartmoor

There is a walk which I love taking in the spring when the countryside is flowering and the air is luminous. The optimism of the season seems to emanate from self just as being in love lends radiance to the world.

So I leave Hay Tor car park and cross the downs to Hound Tor and come via Heatree Cross and Natsworthy to Wide-combe. Here I head for the Rugglestone, a little pub that stands aloof from the catchpenny age with the mediocre rampant and the old values perpetually under attack. This is one of those pubs of my childhood when Dartmoor was the great Arthurian adventure and I felt ready to draw the sword from the stone. Well, it hasn't changed since the 1940s.

Audrey is a no-nonsense Devonian incapable of making concessions to modern times and trends which bring spiritual bankruptcy to rural communities.

The Rugglestone isn't posh. You can sip cider outside in the sun listening to the clatter of the stream that runs a yard or so away or watch the haymaking in the field opposite.

Inside you'll find something resembling your gran's parlour – wooden settles, wooden chairs, wooden tables, a bar Edward Thomas would have been at home in.

The whole place is pure A. E. Coppard and when I was young I came here in search of Dusky Ruth. Here the mid-Atlantic swilling station with its muzak, wall to wall carpets and wall to wall insincerity runs out of credence. This is Devon and it appeals to the parochial part of me that recognizes the Devonian as an endangered species and the old ways of my kind vanishing beneath an all-pervading tourism.

Here I can find the Devon accent before walking on defiantly to climb Widecombe Hill on the long haul back into the 1980s.

Being a wilderness romantic is OK so long as there is a real anchorage or two among the illusions and mirages of Holiday Land.

The Dartmoor Tor

It wasn't one of those grim granite monuments to a geological age so distant it leaves the imagination stranded. The rock was pale, sunlit and warm. It seemed to have a life of its own, borrowed perhaps from the grass growing along the top of the tor and the scrub trees and whortleberry bushes springing from cracks and gullies.

The jackdaws which nested in holes and crevices in the low but vertical crags provided the jangling voice that is part of the spirit of so many tors, mountains, sea cliffs, church towers and quarries. Nowhere was this long narrow outcrop higher than 40 feet and since boyhood I had climbed every one of its rock walls in an unending apprenticeship to mountain craft.

The south facing crags were beautiful in the autumn sunlight. The orange, green, grey and yellow lichens helped again to create that impression of inner life which many of the more celebrated and spectacular tors lack.

I sat on a grassy terrace close to the cave where I had

Carter

Hay Tor, Dartmoor

bivouacked at all times of the year over five decades. The jackdaws' sky-dance was one of those festivals of joy which address the human spirit. In the air above and around me small black shapes swooped and tumbled and twisted, rattling out their cries.

Every so often one or two birds settled on the rocks close at hand and exchanged 'tchaks'. They were neat and atttractive, sparkling vitality. Their grey napes and blue eyes set them apart from the larger members of the crow family and on the wing their aerobatics were startling. Plummeting down the side of the crag they would brake and twist and vanish into a crevice.

Sometimes I looked beyond the mesmeric whirl of the daws at the landscape I loved and had written into my book *A Black Fox Running*. There was the great tor on the horizon and the hillsides falling into the valley where the brook gushed over pebbles and stones beneath birch, alder, willow and rowan to the ponds.

A heron flapped across my thoughts and with a whirring creak of wings a pair of Canada geese swung over the farmland to splash down on the water. The holly tree in front of the cave was rustling, the daws danced in the sky and jangled. In the valley the leaves were sunset coloured.

Change was in the air but for an afternoon I was part of that timelessness central to animal existence.

CHAPTER SEVEN

The Scent of the Sea

Outer Froward Point

A thin sea mist obscured the Channel but even on this April day the sun was hot enough to turn my face the colour of terracotta.

I sat on Outer Froward Point amongst the bluebells and sea campion where slabs and flakes stood angled away from the easterlies like the vertebrae of dinosaurs.

Shags, cormorants and gulls dozed on Shooter Rock and the Stone. Through the binoculars I saw drowsy heads half-heartedly bow to preen. Every so often the gulls alarmed but the clamour of sea birds floating across the narrow minch was pleasant.

When I arrived the ebb was running and the flat tidal skerries landward of the main rocks were all visible. On these natural 'tables' gulls and oystercatchers were eating shellfish. The piping of waders shrilled through the manic braying of great black backs.

I had found one of those sheltered hollows where a body cooks rapidly in the sun. I sat writing, acutely aware of the waves below and the advancing ridges of light on the water.

Every now and then I studied the Mew Stone. It dominates the northern approaches to the Dart Estuary like one of Mervyn Peake's creations – a gothic castle with two distinct towers.

Often I spot a seal fishing at the base of the rock, harassing conger and pollock; but this day he chose not to appear.

The tide turned and the skerries slowly vanished. I got up, descended the point and did some climbing. The wind was rising and the waves had white crests. Once or twice I thought I had located the seal but the binoculars revealed crab pot marker buoys.

Then at 3pm a touch of drama brought me to my feet again.

A motor boat speeding towards the Mew Stone suddenly went silent. Its engine had cut out and the two-man crew were shouting at passing yachts for assistance.

I had visions of the Torbay Lifeboat speeding to the scene but a sailing dinghy pulled alongside and ten minutes later the motorboat was chugging towards the Dart.

Soon afterwards a pleasure boat passed by and the passengers waved. Before I returned to the writing I saw two specks in the sky between Froward and the Mew Stone.

At first I thought it was a couple of migrant butterflies coming home; but it was a pair of swallows. They flew right over me, twittering to each other. Then they began hawking the steeps for winged insects as if that epic flight was nothing.

Seeing them and listening to their joyful cries made my day.

On the Coast

Calm had given way to bluster and greyness. The brambly slopes were quivering in the wind. A flight of mute swans joined the ducks and waders on the flooded marsh. Along the hillside jackdaws stood on the backs of sheep, winkling out ticks. The black birds and their sudden blue sheen were startling.

Halfway through the afternoon I found myself on the down, breathless from coming up on to high ground too fast. Near the top the mounds of a huge warren were pitted with holes. I turned inland. At the head of the valley a farmhouse was silhouetted on the skyline among cider apple trees, horse chestnuts and pines. A cluster of grey outbuildings and silos stood below it on the hillside. I strolled over the pasture until a copse of oak turned me down into the lane. Under the hedges were solitary campions. Near the top of the lane a farm dog with a dead blue eye watched the sparrows splashing about in the puddles. I looked back into the valley. A horse was grazing in the field below the byre among the cattle. Big heavy South Devons and some Jerseys were munching grass beside the stream. Seaward the sky was clearing to blue.

I came to the wall and looked into the bullock yard. A cow gazed back at me over the half-door of the byre and hens scuffed through the straw litter. Sunlight glinted on liquid excrement and golden brown pools of animal urine. Then I saw the rows of fox pads and stoats' tails nailed to the lintel above the byre door. Someone was working in the loft above the barn. The wind came on strong and lifted the loose corrugated sheet on the linhay and suddenly the downs were shafted with sunlight.

Clifftop Day

Fog was ghosting off the frost-whitened grass on the clifftops. The sea had vanished but I could hear it breaking as it pushed through the rocks below. At regular intervals the lighthouse boomed across the bird cries and the low thrum of fishing craft leaving Tor Bay.

The fog lay like a damp cobweb on my head. Crags and outcrops stood in vague silhouette, emerging or vanishing as the fog thinned or suddenly thickened. Beautiful amongst all this ephemeral beauty was the far-off piping of wading birds flying low over the water.

I sat on the limestone tower waiting for the morning to grow around me. Time passed with a glacial drift and an hour before noon a fine day broke from the fog to reveal a blue sky and sea of dark wrinkled jade. Three anglers slithered down the steeps to the promontory and began to assemble their gear.

Immediately below my eyrie the fulmars glided in hypnotic patterns. Rock doves clattered from their nests or returned to vanish into the buttress that fell vertically a couple of hundred feet to the sea.

Jackdaws rattled off their cries into the hubbub of loomeries where the seabirds went about their business. In the air above the fort a pair of ravens cronked and rolled. Forgetting the absence of wild flowers, butterflies and green grass it was a fine imitation of spring.

I searched the sea for oiled birds but mercifully there was none. Cold, exposure and hunger had claimed the guillemot that had flapped out its misery a day or so before. Oil kills slowly and cruelly, but through my binoculars the water looked clean enough and all the auks on its surface were in mint condition.

I began to draw, thinking of Tunnicliffe, although I lacked

his facility for capturing that sensation of space as well as accuracy of form in black and white. Occasionally I was conscious of human voices above and behind me but with the slow fade-away of day I was left to my own company.

I closed the sketch book and breathed on my fingertips. The cold filmed my eyeballs but I did not want to move. I pulled on my gloves and wrapped my scarf around the bottom of my face, recalling vigils on Hebridean mountains and winter Dartmoor.

Evening of the dog star crumbled to dimpsey and the lights of cargo ships and fishing boats filled the darkfall with nostalgia. Then the sky held the season's hard bright stars and walking around the shoulder of the point I was confronted by Berry Head Lighthouse swinging its arms of light like a giant at his bedtime P.T.

Sunshine on my Shoulders

I was spending a lot of time on the sea cliffs despite the bad back which was taking longer to heal than usual. I could walk swiftly but couldn't run. It was a frustrating state of affairs but Nature refused to be hurried.

I strode along the path from Berry Head under a cloudy sky, knowing the day would eventually become sunny. I shouldered an old fishing bag and carried a shepherd's crook which is my favourite walking stick when the back plays up.

Soon I was passing a long sweep of corn, and the sun was shining now in gasps. Sweating was part of the business for I wanted it to be as it was, long ago. Most of my pleasures in the open air have been hard earned.

Beyond Sharkham Point the climb on to Southdown did not cause any distress. A fortnight without exercise and rather a lot of Guinness had taken the edge off my fitness but I was still in pretty good shape.

On the down I found some of the grass cut to yellow stubble and the sheep very white without their fleeces. Being among farm animals was peaceful. They regarded me benignly or so it seemed. Maybe the shepherd's crook was significant . . .

I went down into the coombe and on to the shingle. Sitting with my back gingerly placed to the rock I ate the homemade pasty and the Granny Smiths. Then I returned by the same route feeling stiff and wondering if my back would make me pay for taking liberties.

Flies swarmed off the great dark-green stands of bracken to greedy on my face. Sheep dotted the steeps between the farmland and the clifftops above Long Sands.

It was hot now and I envied the passengers on the pleasure boats being ferried towards the Dart for tea and buns.

Descending to Mansands I met a German at the stile. He was tall, elderly, pleasant-faced, but he had little English and I had even less German.

'I come from Brixl, ja,' he beamed.

'Brixham,' I smiled.

'It's goot?' He pointed towards Scabbacombe.

'Schoen,' I said. 'Good sheep country. Beautiful.'

'Ja, shoen,' he agreed.

So we parted company and I toiled up the great flanks of Southdown knowing the rest of the walk was easy once I reached the top. 'Sunshine on my shoulders' did make me happy.

Looking back I saw the German waving and I wondered how Nations ever came to war.

On the Head

The high vertical rock of the quarry facing north was shrill with the lay of herring gull chicks. Voices speaking into pleasure boat tannoys echoed round the walls.

Kneeling beside the wild orchids I heard the thrum of bees and smelt the grasses, flowers and the sea. Beyond the shadows of the precipices the sun was hot, with distant Torquay over the water turned to haze and the sea broken into spangles and dazzling pinpoints of light.

I climbed the cliff, examining plants which spend most of their lives in shade. At the top holidaymakers were roasting on the turf. Some looked like strawberry and vanilla ice creams – red fronts, white backs!

Beyond the light stands the Berry Head Coastguard lookout station, and I mounted the steps to meet the auxiliary coastguard Ken Dowding. Ken comes from Kingswear and, for the past seven or eight years, has been manning the station three days or nights a week on different watches.

He is a tall, pleasant man, keen on natural history and ideally suited to what must at times be a lonely occupation.

While the trippers cooked on the grass below and kissed goodbye to a night's sleep, he told me about some of the things he had seen from the station over the years.

Back in September 1983, a little before dusk one evening, he had witnessed the congregation of swallows for the migration flight. Over a thousand birds circled the building and the radio mast, breaking away to go back and forth in restless haste.

After an hour they departed, heading east out to sea, pursued right into darkfall by stragglers.

'I've never seen them arrive in a bunch,' said Ken. 'They usually flutter in in twos and threes.'

Down on the end of the head tourists were glassing the shipping. Four picket boats from Dartmouth Naval College cruised by in single file.

'I had a fox here one night,' Ken continued.

'He came round the back of the station and went under the wire on the edge of the cliff into the brambles. That's the first and last time I've seen him.'

He spoke of the great winter storms, the force tens that send waves crashing over Cod Rock and halfway up the cliffs of the Southern Redoubt.

On a cloudless afternoon, with temperatures in the 80s and the breeze like a draught from a furnace it was difficult to think of wild weather.

Berry Head was in a pleasant mood. Flowers were nodding, birds were drifting high in the blue vagueness of the heatwave and the sea was showing its summer face.

Evenings by the Sea

After the last house had receded not only from view but from memory, I felt the sea cliffs tugging at my innards. The hedges were blurs of campion, dandelion and bluebell but suddenly the afternoon flooded back with a sweep of open fields. Insect chirr gave way to larksong. Beyond Scabbacombe head the sea rushed to meet the horizon.

Oiled guillemot on the shore.

I left the lane and started down the sheep field that was pitted and scarred with burrows and rabbit runs. In the valley the stream flowed brown, holding some of the sky's brightness. It was bordered on one side by a gone-wild hedge of oaks and alders.

I came on to the beach and laid the fire. The driftwood sizzled and spat little white salt bubbles. While the flames grew I swam in the surf and showered under the waterfall. Across the cliff face the fulmars flickered, releasing their staccato cries. Later I would fish for bass or maybe go for a big pollock – anything with lots of meat on it to grill on the wire mesh over the blaze.

Under Scabbacombe Head the guillemot loomery was crowded and busy. Adult birds shuttled from the water to the nesting ledges where the chicks stood in dusky siren suits of down. The cliff faces were a great vertical slum providing breeding space for kittiwakes, razorbills, cormorants and herring gulls, as well as the guillies.

One June night I had slept out on Down End Point. Lying among the thrift and salt grass I was disturbed by a low moaning. The mother guillemots were comforting their nestlings but for a while I saw, behind my eyes, the awful crab-nibbled corpses of drowned sailors hauling themselves up the precipice, moaning and cursing in their search for human prey!

In those days the only paths along the cliffs were by courtesy of local badgers and stray sheep. I forced my way through blackthorn thickets and bracken, glad of my heavy hobnail boots and sometimes using the rucksack to shield my face. But the open stretches were a joy to walk.

Often I went as far as the Dart estuary and back to Scabbacombe, taking private property quietly in my stride. I saw a fox run up the sheer rock face at Ivy Cove, found a kestrel's nest in a hawthorn tree and another hidden behind ivy on a vertical cliff. Then I would slip into my black daps and climb up through my cowardice with no audience to applaud the good moves or listen to my gabbled outbursts of fear.

Yesterday's Sea Cliffs

Shadows filled the Kingston Valley but the top of the sheep field was still rosy with sunlight. Rabbits came out to feed in such numbers the hillside seemed to move. I was too drowsy to fish and my constitution had had only 15 years' preparation for the sort of farmhouse cider I was swigging from the bottle. It was lifting my scalp.

In the dimpsey the fire had a comforting glow. I forked the corned beef and baked bean mess from the saucepan into my face. The surf stood up and crumbled and swished up the beach before sliding back in a flat apron of foam, sounding like a sharp gasp for breath.

Extinction is forever, I reflected gloomily, climbing the cliff on to Scabbacombe Head. The sun had risen and I was thinking of the great auk, gone forever, driven into pens by seamen and butchered for bait and food. One of those goose-sized seabirds with its sparrow wings was brought ashore in Ireland at the beginning of the last century and actually burnt as a witch! Morbid curiosity went with the pimples.

But the other members of the auk family were doing OK.

The guillemots and razorbills were buzzing low over the sea or bobbing about in 'rafts' just offshore.

I discarded the old army rucksack that murdered my collarbones and took out the 30 feet hemp. It was good to have it handy if I ventured on to vertical rock. It made me feel like a real climber. My rock climbing skills had been honed on Berry Head and Fresh Water Quarry during primary school days when gathering gulls' eggs for the table was part of our life.

In my early teens I came to the sea cliffs hopelessly in love with nature. I borrowed books on wildlife from the public library but the countryside provided me with a college education – fine outdoor courses in zoology, botany and ornithology plus advanced woodcraft and the principles of survival.

Most of all, though, was the nameless desire to walk to the nameless place. Sometime, somewhere, I would find myself at the last horizon and everything would be revealed like the end of the Batman serial at Saturday morning cinema.

On the steeps above hidden coves I discovered mallow and kidney vetch. The musk of gorse wafted across noons so hot the only thing to do was wallow in salt water beyond the dark jungles of seaweed.

At the base of the cliffs big spider crabs lurked and the inky fathoms reached out for me like living evil. But there were bright places, too, and against the sky above the cliffs hares sat in the green wheat and the song of larks was the music of drowsiness.

Off Froward Point the seal pushed his head out of the water and the sun caught it with a bottleglass twinkle. Here, on the exposed reef, shags sat contemplating the mystery of the Mew Stone and cormorants stood cruciform, drying their wings.

The winter gales had bitten deep chunks out of the cliffs. At high tide I could lie staring over the edge into sunlit depths where wrasse swam and pout whiting flashed.

Sometimes, tramping the bluebell slopes, I came upon a boggy little goyal full of wild flowers and scrub willow. Then the green woodpecker looped out of its crazy yaffle and fell down the steeps in noisy undulations of colour, fusing the nerves in my fingertips.

Back on the beach, feeding bits of dead bracken and driftwood to the fire, I wrote it all down – the twinkling seal, adders snoozing on the thrift, the drowned rat hanging in its watery limbo, the badger cub in the snare.

Beauty and joy always cancelled out pathos, for the sea cliffs were radiantly alive. Whatever they gave me was an echo of what I carried inside myself.

CHAPTER EIGHT

Wildlife and Birds

In Praise of Badgers

They were lumbering bearlike along paths older than any of our ancient streets. The sows with their slender faces, the larger, bulkier boars – the entire sett commune was out foraging for food. By moonlight they would grub for earthworms, insects and bluebell bulbs.

Every so often a white face with its two black stripes would lift and a nose would read the air. The badgers were innocents in an environment made perilous by man. They trod Nightworld with their senses alert and their dew-spiked fur catching the starshine.

Although they carry a multitude of fleas badgers scratch for the love of scratching and are never really happy unless they are digging.

Digging is essential to their well-being but I love to see them in the moonlit dimpsey raking at the tiny lodgers hidden in their hairs.

Often I'm asked if animals have an inner life. I like to believe they do. Certainly they seem to enjoy fine weather and the companionship of their own-kind. Watch horses rolling and kicking their legs in spring sunlight.

They appear to be happy, and if they are capable of

experiencing joy then they must also at times feel sad. They suffer and cry out in pain, so, unless you are heartless, it is impossible to consider them as mere automata.

Badgers bury their dead and several writers have described 'funerals' in detail, right down to the dragging of the body to a hollow and covering it with earth, leaves and twigs. Throughout the interment the animals involved uttered low, sorrowful cries as if they were grieving.

Exploring old setts where badger diggers had opened galleries and chambers I found bones and skulls. Obviously old badgers die underground and are walled-up in the tunnels or 'ovens'.

Writing a novel about badgers I find myself trying to control my anger whenever I consider the persecution these animals have endured at man's hands over the centuries.

I wonder if we will ever outlaw barbarism and learn to live in harmony with Nature instead of endlessly exploiting it or abusing it.

The sanctity of life should be the principle governing our relationship with other species.

Winter Kale

Frost was masking the reek of the kale. The fox placed his nose with the utmost care to a white powdered leaf and drew some personal information from the musk deposited by another of his kind.

'The poor bugger's hungry,' dad said. The boiled sweet rattled across his teeth and he sighed through his nose.

'Do they eat kale?' I asked, pressing my cold little buzzard's foot of a hand into his glowing fist.

'I've sin 'em chomping blackberries and dung beetles,' he sniffed. 'They'm smart. There'll be foxes in Debn when there idn any humans left to plant or cut kale. I like foxes,' he added absently.

I started jigging about. Orange and blue blossoms had mottled my knees.

'D'you want a pee?' he frowned, 'or have 'ee got St Vitus Dance?'

'My legs are freezin,' I grinned. 'If you had short trousers you'd be hoppin' around.'

He smiled and crouched beside me and briskly rubbed my knees with hands like hot sandpaper.

'OK, dad,' I yelped. 'OK – please, dad – bliddy hell! bliddy hell! My legs are on fire!'

'Thought you said they were cold,' he chuckled.

'Very funny,' I nodded, backing into the kale.

The fox stared across the frost-rimed leaves at us, the vertical elipses of his eyes full of the morning light.

'Let's see what he's up to,' said my father.

Now the dog fox was off, porpoiselike, bounding through the kale without a backward glance until he vanished under the bottom bar of the field gate.

'Well,' dad said, flinging out an arm to stop me. 'That's sad.'

The vixen lay on her side, beautiful under the crumbled whiteness of the morning. She was stiff, contorted, dead. The buckshot had seen to that.

'Idn it just the saddest thing,' dad whispered.

He spat out the sweet and rammed his fists into his overall pockets. 'Bliddy sad,' he repeated.

And his words had frost on them.

Voices of the Wilderness

Walking across the high moor, through the ling and bell heather, I put up a small party of red grouse. They whirred away on frenzied wingbeats, keeping low and vanishing down the coombe. Great thunderheads sailed over the sky from the north and I expected snow before I reached the road. The air held a sinister ache. Another bird exploded from the heather and was gone. Shafts of sunlight hit chunks of hill ahead of me and sheep straggled along the horizon.

I sat on the rock overlooking the river valley and unscrewed the top of the flask and poured the hot sweet coffee. A grouse was crying close at hand – not the textbook 'go-bek, go-bek, bek, bek bek' but a peculiar 'helluy, helluy helluy helluy' – like a Sloane Ranger answering the phone. I had a mental picture of the handsome cock bird with his dark-mottled, rich, red brown plumage and thick red 'eyebrows' and white feet. It was the perfect camouflage for a life spent lurking in the heather.

Red grouse are uniquely British birds closely related to the

Scandinavian Willow grouse. They feed on ling heather (*Calluna vulgaris*), eating the seeds and shoots according to the season. On Dartmoor, where most of the country is between 1,000 and 2,000 feet above the sea, winter weather can be severe. The low, rounded hills offer little resistance to winds whistling down from Siberia; but the grouse are tough and survive even the worst blizzards which blow themselves into folk legend. The birds constantly tread the snow with their feet and escape being buried by drifting.

I thought about the survival business as I passed the bones and dirty scraps of wool which had once been a sheep. Modern science and technology can send an astronaut comfortably to the moon and back, yet a Dartmoor snowstorm can kill the unlucky or the idiotic walker a few miles from the road, while a vole burrows out of the nearby drifts, full of life. Nature is constantly sending its explorers through time on voyages of evolution to ensure the survival of the species.

Against the thunderheads, those great storm clouds of mountain country, the raven was as black as anything I have ever seen. It beat across the valley, occasionally bucking on the wind, losing height only to regain it once more and deliver its deep croaks. Ravens, like crows and foxes, are great opportunists. They scavenge for carrion and clean up the carcasses of sheep and ponies which succumb to starvation and the weather. They attend last gasps and feed on the remains of creatures, leaving the bones to whiten on the landscape. Since boyhood I have always thought there is immense dignity in this process – death in the great hushed wilderness, life continuing, then the slow process of becoming part of the place.

The raven is our biggest crow. It has bulk and strength and a big wedge-shaped bill for the butchery of dead creatures. Without crows and foxes the moor would be a less pleasant upland. Winter after winter I lament the death of neglected livestock on Dartmoor but the ravens and their like thrive on the misfortune of ponies and sheep. Again, I see this as proof of the Compensation Theorem, with its action and reaction working towards balance within nature.

The river was running dirty-brown and white over pebbles and rocks. It thundered over the falls below the pass, kicking up a mist and pale rainbows.

Further downstream in the shelter under the downs the

noise of the wind and the water faded and I heard larksong. The small brown bird was hovering above the Bronze Age hut circles and turf on the bend of the river. As it sang the lark climbed higher. Sunlight flared and disappeared and rain slanted down. I pulled up the hood of my cagoule and tied it under the chin. Rain slammed into me and I followed the sheep-walk beside the river that was wider now. The shower passed and the sun shone, and loosening the hood I heard the thin, far-off mewling of a buzzard.

Flood and Lapwings

I was down in the South West corner of Dartmoor just after the thaw set in with heavy rain and fog. Earlier that morning Burrator Reservoir had provided its usual wildfowl cabaret and the conifers surrounding the water sheltered siskins who often betrayed their presence with cries amplified by the deep bowl of hills.

Towards noon I put the field glasses away and drove to a pub that offers good food and beer. I drank a coffee and tucked into the sort of lunch rabbits drool over. Then I left the car and walked the in-country between Mary Tavy and Peter Tavy where the river cuts through a delicious mix of rough pasture and heath. Snow drifts still clogged the lanes.

Between the drifts the stony surface was awash, ankle-deep in places. Rain fell across the cries of lapwing, that most haunting and poignant of wilderness sounds.

Squelching under dripping trees I thought of other places and those lonely cries which suddenly open heartache. The highland Scots call the lapwing 'Peesiweep' and whenever I catch its high double-note I am in a Hebridean dusk, the smell of dulce and peat smoke prickling my nostrils.

A fortnight of frost and bitter cold had been unkind to those birds. The farmland that provided insects and life had been sealed to their beaks and some died from starvation and exposure. Most fled to the estuaries and survived on the mud flats; a few came to the ponds at Clennon.

The rain lashed down but its noise was lost in the roar of the river. The Tavy in spate was central to the merciless atmosphere of a Dartmoor winter that claimed wildlife and farm stock. Deposited suddenly by the lane on the riverbank I stood in awe of the thunderous melt-water leaping in dirty brown waves, sometimes 8 feet high, on its race down to the Tamar.

The river was flexing its muscles, tearing at the small stone bridge, hypnotic, drugged by its own destructive power – more beast of prey than water. Ophelia would not have sang in that torrent, but much later as I came back to the pub I met the cries of lapwings again and thought now of the spring.

Foreign Thrushes

The sky was full of life. Flocks of foreign thrushes from the high latitudes were flighting across the East moors.

Fieldfares and Redwings – birds from the snowlands north of the Baltic – were settling on the whitehorns to take the poppy haws.

Big, round-eyed, crazy looking thrushes returned my gaze in a way that left me uneasy.

The stony stare held the chill of pre-history. It was reptilean, calculating, alien, and I found myself thinking of ice ages and those endless winters out of which migrations were born.

At dusk the flocks of fieldfares were loud with contact cries: 'chak-chak', loosed from scores of throats. The white flash of their under-wings held the last light of day and they flew over the down to roost in the woods above the River Bovey.

During the day I had seen the tall slender birds with their slate-grey heads and rumps probing the grass of the Houndtor Valley for insects and worms.

They were bigger than the redwings whose distinctive call notes could also be heard in the Dartmoor dimpsey. The thin, high-pitched 'see-ip, see-ip' would stop me in my tracks and bring my head up.

Apart from being the smallest of our thrushes this charming winter visitor has red patches under its wings and on its flanks.

Elsewhere small gangs of native mistlethrushes were slamming into the hawthorns like guided missiles.

Again that wide-eyed, lunatic stare pursued me as I tramped across the heather.

Golden plover and lapwings were on the move beating across silvery-grey reaches of evening while the dog star gleamed above the downs.

Now, as the temperature dropped, I felt my thoughts turning to ice. In the stiffening mires the streams tinkled.

Then the rooks came home to Holwell and the ravens settled on their ledge at the disused quarry. Between the highest tors the stars blazed and pulsed and the sky was full of life again.

Buzzard Country

The morning was as warm as anything a South Devon May can conjure from a spell of light south-easterlies, mist and sunshine.

I had written late into the night so that I would be free to shoulder a pack and walk the coastal path. For nearly a year I had lived my spiritual and mental life inside the novel I was writing but now the book was at the publishers and all the sweat, heartache and joy was fading as a new project took shape in my mind.

But to be free to walk in the sun without that burden was bliss! Yet I still found myself plundering the landscape for images and stopping to scribble in my notebook before Time swallowed the moment.

I walked into the sun alive in all my senses. Clouds of gnats danced under the arching blackthorn and to my left was the English Channel and the gull cries which must have saturated my consciousness at birth. I was born less than a quarter of a mile from the sea in April when the herring gulls were nesting.

Striding along I was astonished to find the path practically deserted where it touched the outskirts of Brixham. Leaving St Mary's Bay I had a glimpse of Mansands beyond the bulk of South Down. Here I passed three elderly ladies engrossed in gossip. Then I was over the stile spitting out gnats and wiping them from my eyes.

Beside the stream in the lap of the coombe the bullocks regarded me from brown, placid eyes. The path was pitted with their sun-baked hoofprints but up on the down the going was perfect and the wind carried the warm, damp stink of sheep.

Perched in the bare top branches of a cliffside tree the buzzard followed my progress. Its globose eyes were eight times more powerful than mine so it could see the spot under my right nostril and the sweat dribbling off my brows.

Loosing a mewl of irritation it flapped out to sea, turned, climbed and found its roundabout of wind. At my feet was Mansands and the stream filling the miniature fresh-water ley behind the storm-surf bank of pebbles.

I was glad to be there, in buzzard country whose corners and goyals hold the shadows of my boyhood and that part of me that is indestructible.

Larksong

A squally shower soaked my head and the rain made the rock treacherous. I was climbing without enthusiasm but willed myself around the high corner into the gulley.

On the buttress below the cormorant ghetto the black-backed gulls had gone in for exclusive highrise development. Rain fell again and powdered away leaving a bright and breezy afternoon.

I sat on a ledge at the Point and was buzzed by jackdaws. They were almost as inquisitive as the fulmars that flickered by, sunlight flashing on white bellies.

Among the withered thrift was scattered storm debris – seaweed, shells, small pebbles. When I was a boy guillemots and razorbills thronged the loomeries of the head but gulls and fulmars have taken over most of the old auk sites.

The pollution of the ocean continued and I felt helpless and frustrated. Cloud shadows stampeded across the Channel and the wind knocked against the dead bracken stabs. I climbed on until a flooded inlet ended the traverse and pushed me up on to the badger path.

The deep clefts dropping vertically to coves were like miniature fjords. Sometimes seals strayed to the shingle but they were rarely seen. The steeps enclosing the coves were loud with gulls.

Foxes had killed a number of roosting birds and bones and wings littered the clifftops. Walking the margins where bracken and farmland met was exhilarating.

The lark song was as fine as anything Bach could offer; but wildlife was most active close to the sea.

So I wandered down the stream in the goyal of blackthorn to the waterfall that splashed through its own rainbow on to a pebbly beach. A buzzard rose from the tideline and flapped silently away.

It was warm out of the wind. Gradually the gull clamour faded. Waves swished through the kelp beds and the larks sang on, faint and unreal over the invisible pasture.

The Beauty of Larksong

One day while a monk was walking the downs a lark began to sing and he stopped and listened, spellbound. When he eventually returned to the monastery he found he was a stranger to the other monks and that he did not know any of them. In bewilderment he told them he was Father Anselm and checking the monastery records they discovered a Father Anselm had been there – a hundred years before.

The beauty of the larksong had rendered time meaningless. My father used to tell me that story on a Sunday afternoon after a lunchtime session at the Torbay Inn. I believe it can be credited to J. M. Barrie, the creator of Peter Pan, although it has a traditional ring about it. My old man could be as maudlin as Barrie after five or six pints of best bitter, but most of his response to life sprang out of a deep love of the countryside and human company. In any case, there is an element of timelessness in larksong. The bird sings throughout the year except in August when the high passionate trilling is absent from the sky.

Often when I walk on Dartmoor something close to timelessness prevails. The extra spiritual dimension brings me alive in all the senses and larksong helps to take me out of myself. To witness the ebb and flow of light in the sky or see the dog star firming to brilliance above the tors is to belong to an enduring splendour. On the moors the seasons represent the eternal and larksong rippling across the autumn day helps create that illusion of forever. With sunshine flying and cloud shadow racing across the windy afternoon it is difficult to feel anything but elation.

Gregariousness is hard to understand if you are by nature a loner, and these days there are so many people walking the moor in large groups we seem to be running out of solitude. Erosion of solitude worries me but there are so many ways

Dartmoor can be diminished: too much noise; too many people moving about together; too many self-serving commercial enterprises whose impact on the landscape is insidious or dramatically obvious. Silt from forestry operations gets into the upper reaches of rivers and covers the salmon spawning beds. A vet's bill could wipe out the profit on the sale of a pony, so some sick animals are left to suffer and die. These are facets of diminishment. Much more obvious is the Big Business development of Big Business agriculture with its new giant barns standing like threats on the skyline. As usual it's a conflict of priorities. Do we conserve or exploit? The moor isn't a museum but there are a growing number of people who love it and wish to protect it from powerful concerns.

Larksong is one of those wilderness voices unconsciously pleading for freedom and all that wilderness implies in natural history terms. It is a pity so few of us understand the language, because everything in the world lives under our mercy. Looking back over all the seasons I have enjoyed on Dartmoor I wonder what, if anything, I've given the place. Caring deeply for a landscape does not sweeten the larksong or 'improve' the sunset. But we can tarnish that beauty or destroy it out of stupidity, greed or carelessness. By remaining faithful to nature we remain faithful to our better selves; and if you are tired of finding the countryside organized for people's amusement or leisure or education or any other reason, it is good to tramp unspoilt wilderness alone, competing with no one, seeking the fulfilment only wilderness can give.

Rain falls and lifts scent off the mires. Bleating mingles with larksong and the sound of running water. A herd of ponies shatter the sun dazzle on the stream. Was that this autumn or last year or in the late 1940s? Much of Dartmoor's magic is changeless – spaciousness, vast skies, acres of desolation. A landscape you love continues giving to you throughout your life. It liberates you from the trivia which bombards urban existence, and Dartmoor provides the opportunity to separate yourself from human activities. Yet when I'm there I don't feel I'm turning my back on humanity – quite the contrary. What Wordsworth had to say about 'the still, sad, music' has relevance up there. It really is a beautiful world and we are part of that beauty; but preserving it is a hell of a job now the Gadarene flight into mediocrity has become a stampede.

With this autumn coming to an end I sat on Rippon Tor and looked back over the South Devon countryside I love. Then I remembered the words of Tagore:

'Every child comes into the world with the message that God does not yet despair of man.'

In spite of everything I remain optimistic.

CHAPTER NINE

Flora

The Hawthorn Tree

It is there not far from the wayside. I leave the Bovey Tracey-Widecombe Road at Harefoot Cross and bear right for Hound Tor. About 200 yards down the road on the right hand side the solitary hawthorn is waiting. The tree isn't remarkable as trees go but it has great appeal and I often find people standing before it simply taking in its beauty.

Maybe its situation has something to do with it. Beyond the little tree is the alpine profile of Hay Tor with Saddle Tor more conspicuous in the south.

For years this particular hawthorn has fascinated me and I've often sat on the turf above it gazing across the head of Houndtor Valley where the Becka Brook begins. Cattle, sheep and ponies visit the tree to rub against the dark grey bark of its bole and one morning as dawn was breaking and I was walking quietly along the verge of the road I saw a fox sitting under it looking eastwards towards the brightening horizon.

The radiant greenness of the springtime leaves gives way to the dark summer foliage and like all hawthorns this little Dartmoor tree is best seen in May or October. The white clustered blossom of May and early June is a delight, striking as it does a note of optimism after a typical late wilderness spring and a long hard winter.

At about that time of year the lapwings are nesting on the mires of the Becka Brook wellhead. Their cries possess all the melancholy of great open places where Nature is still in control but the lovely double notes of the curlew are also heard below Seven Lords Lands and all down Houndtor Valley to the ponds.

The hawthorn stands on the edge of a world designed for mythology. In the autumn when the wine-red haw attract the thrushes that have come south from the high latitudes I've often felt stranded beyond the reach of time. Maybe that's how the tree got there – as a berry dropped from the beak of a fieldfare.

Well, the seasons whirlpool gently around the whitethorn and it continues to help me find peace within myself. On many occasions I've looked on it as a companion and sharing its silence has been rewarding after the din and hurry of the seaside town.

The Hawthorn Hedge

The living world still provides moments of intense beauty just when I'm beginning to despair at the loss all around me.

The dandelion rising from between the paving slabs, the grass growing at the base of the supermarket wall, the peregrine over Trafalgar Square – all are a kind of triumph.

High on my list of memorable experiences is the sight of the hawthorn hedge on the right hand side of the A380 Newton Abbot-Torquay Road as I approach the roundabout to cruise on up Hamelin Way.

This is one of those gnarled and ancient hedges my old dad would have looked at from eyes narrowed with pleasure. The origins of similar hedges can be traced back to the 18th century although many of them have Saxon ancestors.

What I like about this particular line of trees is their wilderness quality. They are an authentic touch of wild Devon on the margins of the road for all to enjoy.

In the late spring I am usually in the Hebrides and when I return the Kingskerswell whitethorn greets me with its blossom. The hedge is also the last thing I see coming out of Torbay on my travels. I cannot imagine it going or tidied up.

It is a glory offering birdsong and fragrance – despite the exhaust fumes. There is no need to cut it back, for such an act of vandalism would impair its dignity.

In an age of carelessness with Nature under threat from all sides the hawthorn hedge is a remarkable tribute to what the living world can achieve, unmolested.

I drive past it and enjoy it and let its beauty take me out of myself. I hope the development planned for the Barton hypermarket won't remove it, yet I fear for it because I know that for many people it has no value in itself.

There is nothing in the accountant's ledger to justify its existence.

The Orchard

South Devon, apple blossom, a blackbird singing and the sun and a shower producing a rainbow. It's difficult to imagine a gentler vision.

Cider apple orchards continue to seduce me possibly because I have long followed the life cycle of the fruit from bud to blossom to apple to scrumpy.

A pint of rough (now blessed with the more respectable title of 'dry') at the winter fireside of a Devon pub can resurrect images of spring. Unashamedly I sometimes tread the romantic's route into a somewhere coloured by the Pre-Raphaelites rather than Tunnicliffe.

But there is a remarkable peacefulness to be found in the lanes which carry you through the springtime orchards, and it seems to intensify as the birdsong fades to mid-summer's hush with the fruit ripening and the grasses and nettles standing high around the trunks.

I love the old trees and the old names of the apples which I'm forever listing – orchard poetry you could call it: Sheeps Noses, Foxes Whelps, Bloody Butchers, Slack Ma Girdles – something more potent than French Golden Delicious.

I like to wander along deep lanes under the crooning of wood pigeons and the wren's loud song to come upon the surprise of an orchard in a coombe. Ideally there will be a glimpse of smoke-darkened thatch between the trees.

Such scenes only require the bugling of domestic geese and the muted banjo'ing of free range fowls to send me into a nostalgia high and memories of school holidays, plagues of cabbage white butterflies and the smell of cow parsley and pigs.

Pigs in an orchard, calves in an orchard, horses in an orchard and a stream winding without haste among the trees – it's a country cameo you can discover anywhere from Shaldon to Newton Abbot, Bovey Tracey to Stoke Gabriel, Rattery to Holne and Dartmouth to East Prawle.

I prefer small orchards bounded by old stone walls with the

grass growing on top of them. Where the cider apple trees are beginning to bow under the weight of the fruit at Yalberton I can still find the classic example.

Give it three months and autumn golds and browns will be lit by little spheres of scarlet, crimson and yellow like Christmas Tree decorations. Then the cider making – aided by French imports.

But I like to think that when I swig a pint of genuine farmhouse rough I'm drinking part of an orchard I know and love.

Snowdrops

Among winter's grim austerity I saw the snowdrops shaking in the wind. Earlier this year some were flowering in the snow and it was difficult to regard them without emotion. For me they represent that inextinguishable force, Life, with its often deceptive strength.

Today those Fair Maids of February were surrounded by green, soon-to-flower crocuses and daffodils. Crouching beside them I thought of that fine wild spirit, Emily Bronte. She must have come upon small surprises of snowdrops on the edge of her moor and experienced a delight similar to my own.

The drooping white, bell-shaped flowers are divided into six segments. The inner three have a bright green spot on the tip. The outer three are pure white.

When I was a small boy my father told me how snowdrops came to the world. I can see the old man now, his face blotched with grog blossoms and his eyes twinkling.

According to him it snowed during Eve's expulsion from the Garden of Eden and she began to cry – not because she felt sorry for herself, but she was sad for the flowers the snow was covering. Looking down from Heaven an angel pitied her, so he caught a snowflake in his hand and turned it into a tiny white flower. Then he flew down and gave the flower to Eve. After she had wiped her tears away she saw thousands and thousands of snowdrops springing from the ground all around her.

The Fair Maids of February remind me of the story and my father and the countryside magic that flooded my childhood.

First Signs

The lane came by a tortuous descent from the pines to the valley floor. In the mud under the hedges toads gave me goggle-eyed glances loaded with concern. Spring comes quickly to the South Devon coastlands although the calendar insists it is still weeks away. The stands of bright green cow parsley and unfurling leaves of elder and bramble were evidence of nature's quickening pulse.

Then I saw the sign I've been waiting for since Christmas. They were among the grasses of the marsh – two celandines, one open, one closed. Side by side they stood like tiny flakes of sunlight.

The first sight is especially poignant because I know they occupied a sheltered corner of Henry Williamson's imagination. Each spring they appear at my feet, gloriously humble memories to that writer who brought the Devon countryside so vividly into my childhood evenings when I crouched over the fire with Tarka and the Crowstarver for company.

Soon the margins of the path through the reeds would be littered with these little milky-yellow flowers. I crouched and saw the raindrops within the corolla as a kestrel tacked along the valley and starlings masked the pasture.

On the cliffs above the point an earth had been excavated among the blackthorns. The skull of a seabird was caught in the bare roots. Men had enlarged the entrance with picks and spades to get at the fox whose stink still hung faintly on the air.

Rabbits broke cover as I scrambled down the cliff to the beach. The cove was far livelier than it had been for months. Gulls had selected nesting sites and prospecting fulmars were among the hordes which rose and screamed at me as I appeared on the headland.

Wind in the Willows

The Libellula dragonflies were clicking and whizzing and tacking across the slack water, picking off the small fry. On wings like polythene they hawked the reaches between the bulrushes and reeds, walled in with scrub willow and alder.

Down low the wind was less than the breath of a child but

the willows were full of breeze. It was whitening the leaves and making the trees sway hypnotically.

The marsh was a beautiful, quiet place in the heart of Paignton's holidayland; but the tourists in the caravans and chalets on the hill above rarely ventured into that secret world of willow, reed and water.

During the late spring and early summer there were purple masses of pyramidal and southern marsh orchids hybridising in the shade of the willows and sallows. Rabbits lived on the margins and waterfowl and small birds made the reed beds and trees their home.

The cries of moorhens would come to me on the wind and often a heron would flap away.

Locals visited the marsh with respect, considering it a privilege to have access to a small piece of untamed country-side right in the middle of Torbay.

Often I sat with my binoculars on the eastern slopes overlooking the marsh, watching the butterflies, birds and small animals as the wind blurred the willow leaves white only to shake them back to dull green again.

During my boyhood this had been watermeadows invaded by marsh and floods. Often I found the sky dark with wild duck on distant windy September mornings of flying leaves and light.

Now the wind sweeps across carefully manicured grass for the marsh and the willows have gone to make way for the Clennon golf range.

Walking across that uniform green blankness I heard the willows whispering again and saw the trees silvering in one of those memories many of us share.

Dogrose Morning

The lawn was littered with cats all of whom wore smiles of sun-drugged contentment. The silver birch rustled and shook its broken shadows over the grass. Across the rooftops white sails emerged or vanished into the haze of fine weather on the Bay. A garden warbler sang.

It was a morning made for bike rides down Devon lanes, so my wife, Patsy, and I fetched the machines from the shed and set off. I was on an old Raleigh that had been built for comfort in the days when things were expected to last. It has three speeds and is beautifully heavy, carrying me at a sedate pace along roads built with everything but fast traffic in mind.

We cruised down the Zoo hill to Tweenaway and on to Collaton St Mary where the Stoke road winds into the countryside. It was a relief to escape from exhaust fumes and noise. Soon the hedges were registering as one splendid, blur of scent – the smell of summer. Just as it is difficult to pick out a particular instrument when a great symphony orchestra is in full song so it was impossible to select an individual fragrance.

High green hedges and banks of grass, a blue sky and birdsong with small hills running to an uncertain horizon and the sound of bicycles swishing through sunlight and shade in glorious free-wheel descent!

There wasn't much of that on the up-and-down way to the village by the Dart; but beyond Whitehill Cottages there were dogroses and the deep violet-blue flowers of tufted vetch.

The climb up from Whitehill had got us off the saddle to push the bikes along the wayside for a close-up of plants which are rarely seen from car windows except as brief flashes of colour; honeysuckle, wild orchids, clovers, lady's lace, red campion, comfrey, moon daisies – from Tweenaway to Stoke Gabriel the hedges offered a display borrowed, it seemed, from the memories of an entire generation.

Summers at the end of the 1940s came to mind. The war was over and nothing was under threat. I suppose that glorious illusion fed our innocence.

We cycled on. Sandwiched between the banks was the warm summery smell of cattle. Beyond Four Cross Lanes the outskirts of the village met the fields. Then it was good to cruise down into the dip past the shops and lean our bikes against the wall outside the Church House Inn.

At that time of the day few holidaymakers were about and we could sit on the little terrace outside and quench our thirsts with nothing but birdsong between ourselves and the moment. Geof Bradford and his wife who run the pub joined us and we spoke of how South Devon had changed.

Behind the words I thought of other occasions in the same place – my old man's beery laugh, Sunday lunchtimes wreathed in cider fumes, euchre in the tiny public bar, accents thicker than clotted cream, tall stories about salmon, River Dart chat, Doris setting down the sleever of ale with a grin.

On our return the dogroses were waiting and the grass was swaying in the wind that was just strong enough to take the sting out of the noonday heat. The yard at Collaton Farm was full of cattle. Their bellowing rose above the traffic din which carried us back to Paignton and the seaside crowds.

A Wealth of Celandines

The northeast wind had become boring. For elderly people it must have been more of a penance, blowing day after day to create Siberian conditions in normally gentle South Devon.

After soaking up a couple of weeks sub-zero temperatures and blizzard conditions on Dartmoor the weather finally got to me and laid me out.

A week or so of feverish coughing and moping round the house began to make me feel sorry for myself but eventually I was strong enough to go out and search for signs of spring.

Milder winters always relent early enough to provide drifts of frail blackthorn blossom and even on bitterly cold days with the snow flailing out of an inky sky the mistlethrush's song can lift hearts close to despair. But for me the celandine is the symbol of hope in a comatose landscape.

So I came well-wrapped up against the wintry blast, with sore hair and a sensation of amazing fragility to the place where I knew I would find the little golden flowers. Since childhood the coombe had provided evidence of Nature keeping its bargain with the eternal continuities to which human life subscribes either willingly or unwillingly.

In the hedge the yellowing hazel catkins and the uncurling leaves of bramble and elderberry defied the black nor'easter.

Despite the artic spell Nature's pulse was quickening and I never doubted that I'd find my celandines. They were there in the grasses of the marshy hollow, their petals spread like tiny flakes of sunlight. Kneeling for a closer look I recalled how important they have been to me since childhood.

Every West Country spring is purchased with its wealth of celandines.

Scents and Smells

When I am abroad or in London or simply out of the country I start summoning up little visions of Devon. The other week, returning from a trip to Town, I found myself cataloguing those scents and smells which the alchemy of nostalgia transforms into countryside and season.

The dark stink of wild garlic creeps into my consciousness whenever I think of Scabbacombe Lane and the walk to Mansands. But it's never the Mansands of today. It's the wild little beach of my boyhood with its pebble banks and flooded marsh and lovely atmosphere of nature in control.

The fragrance of hay is one of those rural clichés yet it presides over the recollection of so many childhood summers when I worked at Grange Court Farm.

The mouldy reek of a sea mist can transport me in a flash from the pub on the Thames to Berry Head. Sea mists are magic. As a small boy I remember standing on Berry Head watching the mist rise from the Channel and curl like a great silent predator over the clifftop to glide across the turf and engulf me. That strange cold smell also puts one in mind of Dartmoor with distance erased and the wilderness suddenly rendered totally desolate. It is a smell that prickles the skin and hollows the gut.

These scents and smells are also Devon – sheep-nibbled kale on a coastal headland; bluebells in a Dartmoor combe; cattle dung in a summer lane; the reminder of rain on a drystone wall; potent oozings from the cider mill; the peat gruel of the high moor; the stink of fox sandwiched between hedges; Widecombe strawberries on a girl's lips; rain on Dartmoor granite; the lovely, frail breath of dog roses rinsed from a hedge top by a summer shower.

Of course, these scents and smells aren't peculiar to my county but for me they are part of the fabric of Devon because this is my place.

Beyond the county borders is the rest of the cosmos but I have been elsewhere in the late autumn and have smelled woodsmoke. Then homesickness has nearly proved fatal.

Throughout my childhood when I returned to my terrace house from Clennon Valley the woodsmoke would waft across dusk and lamplight to feed the impossible longing for something I could never understand.

The sensation rises whenever woodsmoke stings my eyes.

Conservation Bulletin

This green and pleasant land has fewer trees per square mile than any other country in the EEC.

While conifers are stifling some landscapes, few summer-leafing trees are being planted and all over Britain little acts of destruction continue to reduce the deciduous population.

I remain incensed by the felling of more than twenty sycamores a little to the north of Outer Froward Point. I do not feel it was justified.

The copse on the steeps above the cliff enhanced that corner of the coast. The trees were also larders for birds.

The sycamore (*Acer pseudoplatanus*) was introduced from the continent in the 15th century. It grows well in stony soil and has a strong spread of roots which bind it to the ground in the fierce winter gales that blow in from the Channel.

Examine the underside of a sycamore leaf and you'll be amazed at the number of invertebrates lodging there. These are eaten by birds including thrushes, robins, hedge sparrows, wrens, tits, warblers, spotted flycatchers, treecreepers and nuthatches.

So the tree provides habitat and food for birds and the persecution of the species locally as part of Draconian scrub management is unacceptable. In fact, there is far too much evidence of severe 'tidying-up' along the coastal footpath, particularly from Elberry Cove to Brixham. Lopped off branches and the clearing of scrub betray the passage of work teams whose activities are over-zealous.

The municipal park syndrome prevails and these small areas of apparent neglect which are so productive in terms of wildlife habitat are removed. It is a sad example of wilderness management failing to operate sympathetically.

Beyond the parochial considerations trees deserve the utmost consideration. They provide oxygen. To produce their food they take in carbon dioxide and give out oxygen. This throws the destruction of rain forests into grim perspective and suggests the need of a rapid solution to the problem.

The governments of wealthy countries should be paying subsidies to the rain forest landowners busily felling the trees, to encourage the protection of rain forest hardwood and the replanting of areas already lost. Subsidies for grain mountains and wine lakes are acceptable so why not cash grants to solve a serious global crisis?

Rain forests could become tourist attractions but the financial carrots are needed to gain the support of the natives. Perhaps the multi-nationals could sacrifice a small percentage of their annual profits to set the ball rolling. Now is the time to act.

Of course, trees have an intrinsic value, but it would be difficult to ignore them as bird habitat and wildlife supermarkets. The willows and sallows of places like the Hallsands reed beds are rich in invertebrates and, therefore, necessary to insect-eating birds which congregate at the marsh at the beginning and end of their migration flights.

More than 250 invertebrates can be found on the salix. Alders in the same marshy coombe play host to around 90 and the silver birch in my garden accommodates around 225. Hawthorn supports upwards of 140, hazel 75, and a crab apple tree has nearly 100.

The champion is the oak that offers food and board to over 300 invertebrates — spiders, woodlice, caterpillars, weevils, earwigs, flies, etc. Cut down a mature tree and you cut off the food supply of many birds in its vicinity.

I keep on about Elsewheres, but really these places are part of the planners' mythology. When creatures are dispossessed by urban expansion they find it difficult to establish themselves elsewhere. The Elsewheres are already the territories of other creatures and the green woodpecker in residence isn't going to take kindly to the newcomer.

CHAPTER TEN

Tail Corn

Scarecold Evenings

One of Autumn's big attractions when I was young were mam's 'scarecolds'. Whenever I came in freezing after a day of mooching about outdoors I qualified for 'a little something to warm the cockles of my heart'.

The prospect always lent dimpsey a peculiar sort of magic. The excitement would churn in my guts as I trotted up Fisher Street under the wheeze and chuckle of the gas lights, past the Torbay Inn and Wotton's corner shop to the Terrace.

The owls crying from the Convent school beech trees were integral to twilight like the smoking chimneys, bonfires, deserted streets and the fallen leaves littering the pavements.

I would come over the wall into the backyard to land beside the dustbin and the rabbit hutches. I rarely used the gate and my old man said I was half-squirrel and half-tomcat for I spent most of the time in trees and on shed roofs.

After a long day in the fields and woods I never entered our kitchen looking like Little Lord Fauntleroy. Clennon's mud would be caked on my boots, knees and the backside of my trousers. Buttons were always missing and shirts and jackets were always tearing on barbed wire and brambles.

Arriving ravenous I might have been regarded as a domestic

disaster in another household with burrs and spiders in my hair, half the valley under my fingernails and my pockets crammed with autumn's treasure. I brought home some hazel nuts in their husks so they would ripen and retain their sweetness for Christmas, and I rarely failed to pocket a few choice cider apples or bramleys.

Shedding my clothes I would stand in the sink while mam washed me down and polished me ready for the tea table. It was necessary to have me bright pink before I was allowed to the fireside. In those days we had an oil lamp in the living room and a coalfire to summon all the lustrous shades of gold out of the brass fender. Then, as I turned the pages of my book, I would give a little cough and tap my chest with a fist. Mam always took the bait and dad would wink.

'I hope you aren't going down with bronchitis again,' she would frown. 'Pull your chair closer to the fire and I'll get you something hot.'

'You crafty lil' heller,' the old man would yawn.

So the 'scarecold' was produced. A little later mam returned from the kitchen with a mug of mulled cider – farmhouse rough, laced with cloves and ginger, and piping hot.

Afterwards I would glow, the fire would glow, and so would the fender, dad's nose and the cat's eyes.

Those evenings were very satisfactory.

A Good Day

Age really hasn't anything to do with it. The sun was warm although winter still lingered in the wind. I felt alive in body and soul and rejoiced in everything around me. Things came into my knowing with the wonderful clarity of childhood when days in the countryside registered like visions.

Everything around me conspired to make me conscious of the majesty of life; the young nettle leaves; the hazel catkins; the familiar wild flowers pushing out of winter's debris. Larks sang and over the fields came the cawing of rooks. I walked through the sunlight to the gorse thicket on the edge of the cliffs and found the remains of the dog fox the hunt had killed some weeks ago.

At primary school we had sung 'Morning has broken like

the first morning' with a sincerity born of innocence. 'Black-bird has spoken like the first bird' – the lovely, simple poetry of earth, full of truth the instinct can relate to. A buzzard sailed over the great bulk of the headland and the hours passed measured by the ebb and flow of the tide on the rocks below and the coming and going of gulls.

It is amazing the happiness we can find in wild places. When I was a child I wanted to belong to the sea cliffs in every possible way, like an animal, and going home after a day on the coast was a real penance. It was never easy to turn my back on paradise.

The sun set and twilight deepened and the air took on a chill as the evening star hardened. Again that keen sense of being alive in every fibre within the living world overwhelmed me. Behind everything is the inextinguishable force. I looked up at the sky. Sheep bleated, gulls wailed.

As always the world under my feet and all around me was enough.